AN INTRODUCTION TO
THE ARCHAEOLOGY OF CORNWALL

AN INTRODUCTION TO THE
ARCHAEOLOGY
OF
CORNWALL

CHARLES WOOLF
WITH ILLUSTRATIONS BY THE AUTHOR

D. BRADFORD BARTON LTD.
TRURO

First published 1970 by

D. BRADFORD  BARTON LTD.
TRURO CORNWALL

COPYRIGHT © CHARLES WOOLF 1970

Printed in Cornwall by
WORDENS OF CORNWALL LTD., PENZANCE

CONTENTS

page

PREFACE   11

I   INTRODUCTION   13

II   THE STONE AGE   17

III   THE MEGALITHIC PERIOD   23

IV   THE BRONZE AGE   30

V   THE IRON AGE   48

VI   THE ROMAN PERIOD   78

VII   THE DARK AGES   85

BOOKS FOR FURTHER READING   98

INDEX   99

ILLUSTRATIONS

Plate		page
1	IMPLEMENTS OF FLINT	49
2	AXEHEADS	49
3	THE TREVEDDRA BEAKER	50
4	TRETHVEY QUOIT	50
5	THE MEN-AN-TOL	51
6	BRANE ENTRANCE GRAVE	51
7	TREGESEAL STONE CIRCLE	51
8	STANDING STONE, ST. BREOCK DOWN	52
9	CARVINACK BARROW	52
10	CARVINACK BARROW EXCAVATED	53
11	CRIG-A-MENNIS BARROW	53
12	CRIG-A-MENNIS URNS	54
13	THE RILLATON GOLD CUP	54
14	GOLD LUNULAE	54
15	BRONZE AGE AXEHEADS	55
16	RIBBON-HANDLED URN	55
17	THE YOULTON BOWL	55
18	IRON AGE POTTERY	56
19	A SADDLE QUERN	56
20	CAER BRAN HILL FORT	57
21	WARBSTOW BURY HILL FORT	57
22	TREVELGUE HEAD CLIFF CASTLE	58
23	RUMPS POINT CLIFF CASTLE	58
24	COURTYARD HOUSE AT CHYSAUSTER	59
25	THE FOGOU AT BOLEIGH	59
26	ST. MAWES INGOT OF TIN	60
27	ROMAN MILESTONE, GWENNAP	60
28	ROMAN VILLA AT MAGOR	61
29	'INCENVI' STONE, LEWANNICK	61
30	THE ESTUARY AT HAYLE	62
31	THE ST. JUST CHI RHO STONE	63
32	THE CASTLE DORE STONE	63
33	THE KING DONIERT STONE	63
34	ST. PIRAN'S ORATORY	64
35	MONASTIC SETTLEMENT, TINTAGEL	64

ABBREVIATIONS USED IN THE TEXT

Ant. Journ.	Antiquaries Journal.
Arch.	Archaeologia.
Arch. Journ.	Journal of the Archaeological Institute of Great Britain and Ireland.
BM	British Museum.
Bod. Mus.	Bodmin Museum.
CA	"Cornish Archaeology"—annual journal of the Cornwall Archaeological Society.
CM	County Museum, Truro.
CR	Cornish Review.
JRIC	Journal of the Royal Institution of Cornwall.
NC	Naenia Cornubia (Borlase 1872).
OC	Old Cornwall. Bi-annual journal of the Federation of Old Cornwall Societies.
PM	Penzance Museum.
PPS	Proceedings of the Prehistoric Society.
PWCFC	Proceedings of the West Cornwall Field Club.
RTPI	Reports and Transactions of the Plymouth Institute.
VCH	Victoria County History.
WCFC	Publication of the West Cornwall Field Club.

FOREWORD

THE ANCIENT LAND OF CORNWALL IS DISTINGUISHED not only by its most beautiful coastline for it ranks very high in the number and diversity of its field monuments. There have always been some who cherish deeply these relics of prehistoric times and the country that enshrines them. The old lure of the West and the strangeness it excites is still experienced and stimulates a curiosity to know the why and wherefore of the structures—how the builders lived, worked and worshipped. To desire knowledge is a good thing and it is in the hope that the simple presentation of facts in this handbook about the monuments will develop this curiosity into a desire for fuller study through the societies and museums of the County.

I wish the handbook every success in its endeavour to encourage an informed mind and eye, for this brings a greater enjoyment and richness to life.

DOROTHY DUDLEY, M.A., F.S.A.
Correspondent in Cornwall
to the Ministry of Public Building and Works.

PREFACE

MANY BOOKS AND PAPERS HAVE BEEN WRITTEN GIVING accounts of early man in Cornwall; some are of a specialist nature or difficult to obtain, others are out of print. This volume is prompted by the fact that there has never been a simple guide for the enquiring person who has seen ancient monuments about the county, who knows nothing about them, but who wishes to commence learning something of the people who built them, why they did so, and who occupied Cornwall in past ages. It is written entirely for the uninitiated in the briefest of terms and its purpose is not to propound original thought or put forward new theories.

To assist the reader who wishes to pursue a particular matter, frequent references have been given within the text which indicate where more detailed information may be obtained. To the same end, a short list of books for further reading is on page 98 and following each chapter is a list of sites to see. By finding as many of these as possible, the story will be brought to life, the Cornish countryside appreciated, and the feeling of the mystery of the past experienced. It must be stressed that good maps are essential, the obvious choice being those produced by the Ordnance Survey. These carry a wealth of information and through them, sites can be pinpointed by means of the references given. The scale of one inch to the mile generally suffices but the two-and-a-half inches to the mile are preferable for really detailed study.

Archaeological knowledge is gained through excavation; readers should support the Cornwall Archaeological Society by becoming members, thus assisting it in its work. By so doing, their own knowledge will be increased through its annual journal and other publications; they can also take part in excavations which the Society arranges each year.

I am grateful to many friends for their often unwitting encouragement to study the archaeology of Cornwall. In particular I am indebted to Professor Charles Thomas, M.A., F.S.A., who first introduced me to the subject through adult education classes many years ago. To Miss Dorothy Dudley, M.A., F.S.A., correspondent in Cornwall to the Ministry of Public Building and Works, for much guidance, for kindly reading my manuscript and writing the foreword. I thank the Royal Institution of Cornwall for allowing me to photograph pre-historic objects in its museum at Truro; particularly its curator Mr. H. L. Douch, B.A., and his assistant Mr. R. D. Penhallurick, B.A., for their characteristic patience and assistance with the work incurred in doing this. The real incentive to produce this book came from the numbers of people seeking knowledge of Cornish archaeology who have attended my lectures. Their interest has been most stimulating and it is to them that the following pages should be dedicated.

I leave the reader with a thought by Graham Hutton, taken from his *English Parish Churches* (1952), which so much expresses the feelings I have experienced during many years exploration of Cornish antiquities—"The tale of beauty, the voices of stones and talk of the past can only be heard by those who take pains and patience. When heard, they are unforgettable".

CHARLES WOOLF
Bard Den Delynyans of the Cornish Gorsedd

Newquay
Cornwall
1970

I

INTRODUCTION

The dictionary defines archaeology as "the study of antiquities, especially the pre-historic period", the word coming from the Greek "arkhaios" meaning 'ancient'. From the definition, it may be seen that it is not necessarily the study of pre-history, which in southern England, ends with the coming of the Romans in A.D. 43, that is, when written history commenced. Thus, there is today, the subject of 'Industrial Archaeology', the recording and examination of industrial monuments of perhaps only a hundred years ago. As far as this book is concerned, however, nothing later than A.D. 1000 will be considered. The methods used in archaeology —excavation and the studying of remains uncovered—enables archaeologists slowly to piece together the history and ways of life of people who existed before written records were known.

THE STUDY OF ARCHAEOLOGY

Many study archaeology because they find it of intense interest —rather like piecing together a vast jig-saw puzzle. Apart from the out-door physical joy of an excavation, there is always the expectation, often realised, of making an unusual discovery or one which accurately dates the site, or indicates the people who lived there. Similar finds may have been made in another country and thus the movements of people can be deduced. Through archaeology, the development of the human race can be followed; from cave-dwellers to farmers and traders, from man clothing himself in animal skins to learning the art of weaving cloth, inventing methods of extracting metals from their ores or machines like the potter's wheel. It is gripping to see the picture grow as the pieces are placed together both from work in the field and research in the library.

CORNWALL AND ARCHAEOLOGY

In spite of the ravages of time, weather and the activities of modern man, Cornwall is very rich in pre-historic remains. It is said, that for its size, West Penwith (the Land's End peninsula) has a greater concentration of these than any area in the country. It should be remembered that when people dwelt in stone huts in Cornwall, parts of the eastern Mediterranean were highly civilised. Men sailed from there, following the west coast of Europe to Brittany and then on to Ireland and the west of Scotland. Mid-way between Brittany and Ireland, the rocky peninsula of Cornwall was in their path; this made it a convenient stopping-place and further, there were supplies of tin to be obtained. Some of the voyagers settled here, bringing with them an infusion of new ideas from their homeland. They lived and died in Cornwall, leaving behind remains of their dwellings, the tools they used and their burial-places.

Until the coming of the railway in the last century, Cornwall has always been difficult of access by land, for in the east of the county the river Tamar, the moors and the valleys surrounding them, form natural barriers. Hence, for centuries, the county has remained relatively undisturbed except for mining and agricultural operations; pre-historic remains have had a reasonable chance of preservation, therefore.

PRESERVATION OF ANCIENT MONUMENTS

The present-day encroachment on the countryside by urban dwellers, agriculture, road improvement schemes and the like, presents a serious threat to the preservation of ancient monuments and constant vigilance is called for. Fortunately, the more important of them are now in the protection of the Ministry of Public Building and Works (here after referred to as the 'Ministry' in the interest of brevity). This will ensure their continued preservation against vandalism, for it is an offence to damage a scheduled monument. It must be stressed, however, that even if a site is not scheduled, no attempt should be made to excavate it, for such work must only be undertaken by those with the necessary skill and capable of making a methodical report of the results. Casual diggers can do irreparable damage with a corresponding loss of knowledge so vital in piecing together the life of early man in Cornwall.

THE SCENE

It is important to look briefly at the scene in which Cornish archaeology is set, for this influenced the lives of early people just as it does ours today.

Cornwall has a backbone of granite highlands which help to give the county its elongated shape. These are known as Bodmin Moor, Hensbarrow Downs (north of St. Austell), the Carnmenellis hills (south of Redruth) and the moors of West Penwith where the granite reaches the sea at Land's End. The land surrounding these highlands consists roughly of a plateau which has been cut into valleys by streams making their way to the sea, their direction of flow being approximately north and south, that is, across the breadth of the county. The general trend of modern travel being east and west, the valley alignment has provided road and railway builders with many problems. In the days of pre-historic and early historic man, however, travel tended to cross the breadth of the county from coast to coast and trackways followed the line of the valleys. Even today, after centuries of de-forestation, these valleys are well-wooded, but in past ages the woodlands were much denser, so much so that early man, with his primitive tools, was unable to clear them. Hence, most of the remains of the remote occupants of Cornwall are to be found on high land where they could live more conveniently. It might be remarked that the climate was milder in those days. When standing in the heart of Bodmin Moor or on parts of West Penwith, the scene presents a landscape much as early man saw it. As tools improved and agriculture was introduced, the lower regions were cleared and man moved down to more sheltered conditions—a process which is still taking place.

The action of the sea on the coastline is also of importance. In past geological time, the sea invaded the estuaries of many rivers thus providing sea-going travellers with easy entrances to the county. On other parts of the coast, softer rock has been eroded whilst harder has withstood countless storms. In this way, numerous sandy bays, terminated at each end by a rocky headland, have been produced. These headlands, like the moors and flooded estuaries, have played their part in the settlement of ancient man who was obliged to utilise the natural geographical features of the landscape for his requirements.

ARCHAEOLOGY AND TIME

The following time scale sets out the periods commented upon in this book. It should be appreciated that in pre-history, dates can be only approximate; in addition, one period did not end, and a new one commence, at once. There was an overlap as one dissolved into another, features of two ages appearing at the same time. Moreover, as a result of excavation and the knowledge gained from it, dates are constantly changing. Those which follow are at present accepted in Cornish archaeology.

	In Cornwall begins about
STONE AGE	
Paleolithic (Old Stone Age)	15,000B.C.
Mesolithic (Middle Stone Age)	6,000B.C.
Neolithic (New Stone Age)	3,000B.C.
BRONZE AGE	
Early Bronze Age (E.B.A.)	1,800B.C.
Middle Bronze Age (M.B.A.)	1,400B.C.
Late Bronze Age (L.B.A.)	900B.C.
IRON AGE	
Iron Age 'A'	550B.C.
Iron Age 'B'	350B.C.
Iron Age 'C'	150B.C.
ROMAN PERIOD	A.D.45
DARK AGES	A.D.410 to A.D.1,000

II

THE STONE AGE

THE PERIOD OF PRE-HISTORY TERMED THE STONE AGE is so-called because, apart from wood and the antlers of deer, stone was the principal material known to man with which to make his implements. The names of the eras into which it is divided, Paleolithic, Mesolithic and Neolithic, all have a suffix derived from the Greek word for 'stone', which is 'lithos'. Therefore, words containing 'lith' or 'lithic' have some reference to stone. For example, megalith=a large stone, microlith=a very small stone, monolith=one stone, usually standing vertically. Note should also be made of the Cornish word 'men', which appears in many words and names, and which also means 'stone'. (For example, menhyr, or menhir=the same as monolith; Men-an-Tol=the stone with a hole in it; Men Scryfa=the written stone). The beginnings of the names of these three eras are also Greek; 'palaios'=ancient, 'mesos'=middle and 'neos'=new.

FLINT WORKING

Most of the earliest tools of man were made from flint—a material which can be made to produce very sharp edges or points and thus useful in the manufacture of weapons, scrapers and knives. Early man was very skilled in fashioning flint (*plate 1*) and his expertise would be hard to equal today using only the means at his disposal. Flint can be worked in three ways; by striking it a blow, by pressure-flaking or by polishing. In the first method, a flat surface (the striking platform) of the nodule is given a sudden blow which causes a portion to split off. Flint is curious in that whenever this happens, the same fracture surface is formed. Immediately below the point of striking, a rounded, raised lump appears (the bulb of percussion) and beneath this waves (ripples) form in the flint. By continual striking, smaller or larger flakes, which will have very sharp edges, can be produced with care. When it is no longer possible to use the nodule because of its unsuitability or diminishing size, it is discarded and what is left is

17

termed a 'core'. Pressure-flaking is used for finer work, the method being to exert an even pressure on the tool to be worked by means of a second, blunt piece of flint. This causes a fragment to fly off and by this means small weapons like arrowheads could be exquisitely shaped. Polishing is just what the word suggests—a laborious method of shaping and sharpening which was a development of later Neolithic man. Where men sat working flint there was always a great deal of waste material and it is often possible to find the site of a flint manufactory in Cornwall (for example, Trevose Head). There being no chalk in the county, flint is not a local material so it may be asked from where early man got his supplies. It can be found as beach pebbles, principally in Mount's Bay, presumably brought there by the sea. Alternatively, it could have been imported from Devon where ample supplies occur at Beer Head.

PALEOLITHIC MAN

As the time scale shows, the Paleolithic or Old Stone Age existed in the very dim past. Man at that time was a cave-dwelling hunter and extremely primitive. There are no remains of Paleolithic man in Cornwall and the county at this remote period would seem to have been uninhabited. An axehead of Paleolithic type was found at the Lizard (CM) but as some consider this single find of doubtful provenance, too much store should not be set by it.

MESOLITHIC MAN

The occupants of Cornwall during the Mesolithic or Middle Stone Age were very few. As they were prodigious workers of flint, it is the remains of this industry which identifies their living sites. These are mainly coastal and those so far known include Sennen, St. Levan, Goonhilly, Trevose Head, Dozmary Pool and Hudder Field, near Camborne. Their characteristic implement was a blade of flint about 1 inch long and very sharp both in edge and point (*plate 1a*). These are known as 'microliths' or 'pygmies' and it is thought they were used by inserting them in a stick to form a cutting or barbed weapon. Since similar sites to the Cornish are found on the west coast of France and in Brittany, it would appear that these people came from these places thus providing the first evidence of contact between them and Cornwall which existed throughout the ages. Since no pottery of this period has been found it would seem that they had not developed this art.

NEOLITHIC MAN

In the Neolithic or New Stone Age are encountered the first really interesting people from the Continent, for they brought with them quite new techniques. They had developed a very efficient stone axe (*plate 2c*) with which they were able to clear forests and for the first time make any alteration to the natural landscape. Unlike their predecessors who had hunted food, they had learned to produce it by clearing the land and ploughing it. They brought with them cows, sheep and dogs; in other words, they were our first farmers. They were potters and like other cultures, produced pottery of a distinctive kind which was very simple, undecorated and with rounded bases to the vessels. Their stone implements consisted of axes, mace-heads and beautifully made leaf-shaped arrowheads (*plate 1b*). Mace-heads (*plate 2b*) were flat, circular stones with a centrally-drilled hole which enabled them to be fixed on a stick hammer-wise. These continued in use into the Early Bronze Age as a weapon, a symbol of office or both.

AXES

Axes dating from this period are of fine shape and some are beautifully polished (*plate 2c*). They were either of flint or local greenstone which is a hard, basic, igneous rock. It is evident that there was considerable trade in these, for axes of Cornish stone have been found as far away as Essex. The place of origin of an axe is determined by microscopic examination of the stone of which it is made—a science known as 'petrology'. Axe manufactories can thus be determined. At the County Museum, Truro, many axeheads are displayed which are annotated, showing the groups to which they belong. However, study of axes is a specialised one beyond the intention of this book.

SITES

Neolithic peoples occupied hill-tops, their best known being Windmill Hill in Wiltshire. As far as is known at present, the only hill in Cornwall they lived on was Carn Brea at Redruth. This fact was discovered by accident when the Iron Age hill-fort there was being excavated in 1895 so there well may be other sites. The presence of Neolithic folk on Carn Brea was shown by the large number of leaf arrowheads found as well as a few pieces of Neolithic pottery. (CM)

POTTERY

Before proceeding further, some consideration must be given to the important subject of pottery. Earthenware vessels in early days were shaped by gradually being built up from their base. By the Iron Age, the use of the potter's wheel had been discovered. Early pots were simply decorated by criss-cross scratchings or by indentations in the soft paste by means of the joint of the leg of a bird, a fish bone, the thumb nail or the fingers. As the centuries pass, more sophisticated designs evolve such as Glastonbury ware (q.v.) of the Iron Age. The paste used for early pots was often coarse and gritty and the walls of the vessel thick because of the way in which it was made. Earthenware is fragile and breakage was frequent; when this took place, the pieces were thrown aside, trodden underfoot or otherwise relegated to the soil. An archaeologist conducting an excavation always hopes to find sherds of pottery; a complete pot would be better but to unearth one of these is rare. Each culture produced its own distinctive ware, so by means of it he can give a date to the site under excavation just as an antique dealer can distinguish a Victorian porcelain figure from one of earlier or later date. Three or four well-defined pieces may be sufficient for this purpose, as at Trewey-Foage (q.v.) but the three thousand found at Bodrifty (q.v.) give the additional information that the site must have been occupied by a number of people over a long period. Pottery can, therefore, tell a true story about a site and its study is so vital that some have made it almost a life's work.

MONUMENTS

As well as providing the first pottery known, the Neolithic people left behind the first outdoor monuments still to be seen. The best known of these are outside Cornwall—Stonehenge and the great earthwork at Avebury, both in Wiltshire. They consist of a flat, central area surrounded by an earthen bank which has a ditch *inside* it. At Stonehenge, the bank and ditch have almost disappeared but at Avebury it is visible beyond doubt; the central

arena of both these monuments is occupied by large standing
stones. Since the ditch is inside the bank, these earthworks could
not have been designed as defensive positions similar to those of
the Iron Age (q.v.); it is thought that they were used as places for
some ceremonial or religious occasion and they take the general
name of 'henge' monuments from the most famous of them all,
Stonehenge.

There are considered to be three henge monuments in Cornwall.
On the southern slopes of Hawk's Tor, close by the A30 trunk
road on Bodmin Moor, are the Stripple Stones—a stone circle

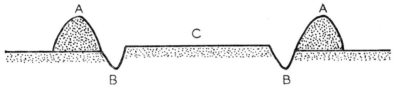

Section of typical Henge Monument.
A   Banks   B   Ditch   C   Open area for ceremonies

surrounded by a ditch and bank reminiscent of a small-scale
Avebury. Then there is Castlewitch, near Callington, now situated
in a cultivated field, with the result that the bank and ditch has
largely been ploughed out but the original construction is clearly
visible. The most easily reached of the three is Castilly, Lanivet.
This is only a very short distance from the A30—in fact, visible
from it. It has to be admitted that an excavation by the Cornwall
Archaeological Society in 1962 failed to prove that it is indeed a
Neolithic monument (CA 3) but even if it has been put to other
purposes in the course of time, in view of its perfect 'henge'
lay-out, it is easy to adhere to the tradition that it is a monument
of this class.

BEAKER FOLK

About 2000B.C., Britain experienced an invasion by "a small
group of the dynamic Beaker Folk . . . a race of powerfully-built,
short, ugly men and women with round heads and prominent
brow-ridges" who originated from Spain (Aileen Fox, *South West
England*). These people buried their dead individually in a pre-
natal position, that is, with legs tightly drawn up and arms bent.

These are known as 'trussed' burials and they took place in small, round barrows twelve to twenty feet in diameter—very different, therefore, from the great barrows of the Bronze Age (q.v.). The name 'Beaker Folk' has been given to them because of their practice of placing with the dead small, characteristically-shaped pots or 'beakers' (*plate 3*). These are quite small, being from six to eight inches in height. It has always been thought that the Beaker Folk were unknown in Cornwall but the discovery of three beakers in the county in recent years leads to a re-consideration of this belief. These people brought with them a new form of axe head which had a hole drilled in it to receive its shaft (*plate 2d*). In earlier times the head had been bound to the handle with thongs and was less efficient on that account. They also introduced an advanced form of arrowhead (*plate 1c*) which continued to be used into the Bronze Age. Their graves have also produced knives of copper which indicates that they had a knowledge of metal-working; thus their advent in Britain may be considered as leading into the coming Ages of metal as opposed to stone. Meanwhile, the Stone Age may be seen as a period when Cornwall was very sparcely populated by nomadic peoples who were eventually replaced by new-comers who had learned the elements of settled life and agriculture.

III

THE MEGALITHIC PERIOD

The megalithic period (megalithic comes from the Greek 'megas'=great and 'lithos'=stone) has been termed a 'period' and not an 'age'—hence it does not appear in the time scale. In dating it is roughly defined as falling between 2000B.C. and 1500B.C. and is a period when north-west Europe, the west coast of the British Isles and Ireland received travellers from Spain, Portugal and southern France, these bringing with them an era of tomb-building—tombs which in many instances were built with un-hewn stones of great size. Ireland is particularly rich in these, as are the Isles of Scilly. Cornwall can offer many examples of megalithic tombs which, for the simple purpose of this book, can be divided into two types, namely, 'chamber tombs' and 'entrance graves'. Most of them are concentrated in West Penwith.

Chamber Tombs

Chamber tombs are burial mounds which contain a stone chamber in which the dead were laid. The most conspicuous of them are known as 'cromlechs', or colloquially as 'quoits'. There are nine of these in the county, the size of some of the stones used in their construction causing wonder at the amount of labour which went into their building. They consist of a varying number of upright stones which support one laid horizontally across them; this is known as the 'capstone'. Trethevy Quoit, St. Cleer, is a good example to visit for it is well-preserved and presents a dramatic appearance since the capstone slopes at an apparently precarious angle. The historian Norden, writing in 1598, describes it as "a little howse raysed of mightie stones, standing on a little hill within a fielde"—just as it can be seen today (*plate 4*). It is one of two quoits which have a pair of chambers, these being formed at Trethevy by an upright stone which has a piece cut from one corner to provide a passage between the two. This might have been done to allow the spirit of the departed to escape or some

23

food may have been placed at the hole for use in after-life; there is no known reason for its presence, however. The second tomb which has an ante-chamber is Zennor Quoit, which is found high on the moors above the village of Zennor. This is of very large dimensions but the capstone has fallen to the ground at one end due to the removal of stones for utilitarian purposes. A sketch by William Borlase, made in 1754, shows the quoit complete (NC). Mulfra Quoit, in Madron parish, shows a similar defect, but standing on the top of Mulfra Hill it presents a very impressive sight. Lanyon Quoit, not far from Mulfra, is the most accessible of all for it stands on National Trust property alongside the moorland road from Morvah to Penzance. Only three uprights carry the large capstone and it forms the 'tripod dolmen' of older antiquaries. In 1815 a gale caused it to collapse but it was re-erected as it is seen today. Previously, it is reputed to have stood much higher. Another tripod dolmen was at Caerwynnen, Pendarves, near Camborne; this collapsed for the second time in 1967 and has not been erected again. Fortunately, there are photographs available which record its appearance. Another quoit which has fallen is West Lanyon, across a couple of fields from Lanyon. By the size of its capstone this must have been an impressive monument originally; now, it is scarcely worth a visit. Lanivet Quoit, near Trebyan at Lanivet, presents the same appearance but must likewise have been a fine monument. Back in West Penwith, near Chun Castle (q.v.) is Chun Quoit. This is very small but of striking appearance, with a large capstone balancing on quite small supports. This is complete and is well worth visiting, being reached by a delightful walk across the moors high above the sea; the important castle can be seen at the same time. Finally, there is the out-lying Pawton Quoit in St. Breock parish near Wadebridge. This is on cultivated land and close approach is not always possible, for example, if the field in which it stands is in corn, but even a distant view makes the effort taken in finding it worthwhile. It stands on a conspicuous mound and its deep capstone, from 2 ft. to 2 ft. 3 ins. in thickness is most unusual.

On visiting quoits one might well wonder how they fulfil the description "burial mounds which contain a stone chamber". It is certain that quoits were at one time enclosed in such a mound and in the case of Trethevy, Pawton and Lanyon, the remains of it have been seen and clearly delineated. As Chun Quoit is approached in early Summer when growth is fresh, bracken clearly indicates the disturbed ground which the circular mound over this monument once occupied. These large mounds of earth and stones were very tempting to farmers who wished to build hedges and spread earth over their fields as will be seen in the chapter on the Bronze Age; this probably accounts for their destruction although, fortunately, the stone chambers have been left.

The dating of these monuments is difficult as far as accuracy is concerned. Such obvious structures have always attracted attention resulting in pillage over the years. There is, therefore, nothing for the modern archaeologist to find in them which might be useful to assist in dating. He has to rely on reports of finds many years ago and these are not always well documented. For example, in 1881 a farmer broke up two slabs of Zennor Quoit *by blasting*, a very different technique from that practiced today. He found a whetstone and a portion of a pot, both of which can be related to the Bronze Age; a whetstone certainly would not be necessary if there were no metal to sharpen on it. A date of 1600–1500B.C. is given for this quoit.

One monument in West Penwith has attracted much attention from time to time, the Men-an-Tol (*plate 5*). This consists of two standing stones and one between them, on edge, with a hole about twenty inches diameter cut in it. Many uses have been attributed to it by serious-minded scholars as well as the local belief that children passed through it will be cured of rickets, and older people cured of a crick in the back—hence another name given to it "The Crickstone". It is now considered that it is the remains of yet another double-chambered tomb similar to Trethevy. At Tolvan farm, Constantine parish, is the Tolvan Stone. This is now in the farmyard but is reputed to have been brought there from not far away where it was found amongst other large stones. This is a very massive stone with a hole sixteen inches in diameter and is said to have similar curative properties to the Men-an-Tol and like that monument, is thought to be part of a quoit.

ENTRANCE GRAVES

Entrance graves are considered to be rather later in date than chamber tombs, the dating 1700–1400B.C. being assigned to them. In design, they consist of a well-built stone passage running from the outer edge of the mound to its approximate centre, the stone-work not fully enclosed in the mound as chamber tombs. They are particularly numerous on the Isles of Scilly, forty being known there compared with about a dozen in Cornwall. As the Cornish graves have been denuded of their contents, the results of excavation on Scilly gives some indication of their use. An examination of Obadiah's Barrow, on the Island of Gugh, produced pieces of pottery and cremated human remains. Similarly, the excavation of a tomb at Knackyboy Carn, St.

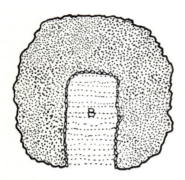

Plan of Entrance Grave.

B   Burial chamber

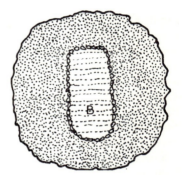

Plan of Chamber Tomb.

B   Burial chamber

Martin's, produced no less than twenty-two urns, implying cremation, in only half of the grave. It would appear that the entrance grave might be the fore-runner of the modern vault. Cremation, as will be seen, comes much later in the time scale. All the Cornish entrance graves occur in West Penwith; this is the part of Cornwall nearest to Scilly and thus it might well be that their builders were immigrants from there. A solitary example may be seen in a field on Pennance farm, Zennor (within sight of the St. Ives—Land's End Road) and another at Brane, Sancreed (*plate 6*) which is quite near Carn Euny settlement (q.v.) There is a very accessible group at Treen, not far from the Gurnard's Head hotel. In 1967, the Ministry excavated what appeared to be a simple barrow at Tregiffian, St. Buryan. The work revealed, however, that it contained a chamber tomb. The excavation was carried out at the request of the county authority who wished to re-align a road which was deviated by the barrow. In view of this important discovery, the tomb has been preserved and may be seen at the roadside.

STONE CIRCLES

Stone circles are classed as megalithic monuments and consist of a varying number of rough, up-standing stones arranged, as the name suggests, in the form of a circle. The average diameter of the twenty-one circles in Cornwall is about ninety feet, the stones themselves averaging five feet in height. In most cases, some of the stones have fallen and others have been removed; allowing for these, the average number of stones to a circle is about twenty-four, although this figure does not include the circles at Fernacre and Stannon which have sixty-four and seventy-six remaining stones respectively. The reason for which these circles were erected is obscure, although the suggestion that they were used for religious or ceremonial purposes is a probable one. When they were built is not easy to decide for any excavations, for example at the Hurlers (unpublished) and the Stripple Stones (Arch. 61, part 1), have only revealed a few flints and have provided little further information about them. The Hurlers are dated by the Ministry to 1500 B.C. All the circles are worth visiting, for standing on open moorland as most of them do, they demand a pleasant walk to reach them and invoke the "feeling of the mystery of the past".

Undoubtedly the best-known of Cornish circles is at Rose-modress, St. Buryan, for it stands in a field beside a busy road. This is marked on the Ordnance Survey map as "The Merry Maidens"—a reference to the legend that they were originally little girls who were turned to stone for dancing on a Sunday. This also gives rise to the Cornish name "Dawns Men" (dancing stones). Nearby are two large menhirs named "The Pipers", these being said to represent the two men who were playing the music to which the children danced. It is interesting to note that the Merry Maidens form an almost perfect circle, so accurately are the stones placed. An interesting point about the circle at Boscawen-Un, also in St. Buryan parish, is that it has a single standing stone within it. The only other comment called for refers to the Hurlers, Linkinhorne parish. They stand on the open moor near the village of Minions in the midst of a former mining area and comprise three circles side-by-side, a fact rather difficult to realise from the ground, especially as many stones are missing. They receive their name from a similar legend to that of the Merry Maidens except that in this case the stones represent men petrified for hurling with the silver ball on a Sunday—a reference to the ancient Cornish game now perpetuated at the town of St. Columb on Shrove Tuesday.

STANDING STONES

Standing stones (monoliths, longstones, menhirs), being extremely large, are also usually included amongst megalithic monuments; they are widely distributed in the county (*plate 8*). The reason for their erection is not known but they may well have had a religious or commemorative purpose; some certainly mark burials for an excavation at the base of the menhir at Try, Gulval, produced a small, handled beaker (CM). Similarly, at Tresvennack in Paul parish, one large urn and a small pot were found (CM). Another at Kerrowe, Zennor parish, was excavated in 1935 and the soil at its base was found to be "black, heavily burnt and full of charcoal". Standing on a little heap of charcoal were two pots, one placed inside the other, six inches and four-and-a-half inches high respectively (CM). There were no human remains but there was clear evidence of a burial in association with the pots. (PWCFC Vol. 1 New series No. 2). Excavation at others has proved fruitless although these might have been rifled in the past by those in search of gold treasure which is often thought to have been buried at their base.

To summarise, it would seem that the Megalithic period represents a culture superimposed on the time scale which extends from the end of the Neolithic period into the Early Bronze Age and is one which affects the westermost part of Britain only.

STONE AGE and MEGALITHIC PERIOD SITES TO SEE

HENGE MONUMENTS	Parish	Map reference
Castilly	Lanivet	186.031628
Castlewitch	Callington	186.371685
Stripple Stones	Blisland	186.144752
CHAMBER TOMBS		
Caerwynnen	Camborne	189.650373
Chun	Morvah	189.402339
Lanyon	Madron	189.430337
Lanyon, West	Madron	189.423338
Lanivet	Lanivet	186.071628

Mulfra	Madron	189.452354
Pawton	St. Breock	185.966696
Tregiffian	St. Buryan	189.431245
Trethevy	St. Cleer	186.259688
Zennor	Zennor	189.469380

Associated with these, being considered as part of a chamber tomb

| Men-an-Tol | Madron | 189.427349 |
| Tolvan Stone (in farmyard) | Constantine | 190.706282 |

ENTRANCE GRAVES

Brane	Sancreed	189.401282
Carn Gloose	St. Just-in-Penwith	189.355313
Chapel Carn Brea	St. Just-in-Penwith	189.386280
Pennance	Zennor	189.448375
Treen	Zennor	189.438371
Tregeseal	St. Just-in-Penwith	189.381322

STONE CIRCLES

Boscawen Un	St. Buryan	189.412274
Boskednan	Madron	189.434351
Duloe	Duloe	186.236583
Fernacre	St. Breward	186.145800
Hurlers, The (three circles)	Linkinhorne	186.258713
Leaze (two circles)	St. Breward	186.137773
Merry Maidens	St. Buryan	189.433245
Nine Maidens	Wendron	189.681365
Stannon	St. Breward	186.126800
Tregeseal	St. Just-in-Penwith	189.387324
Trippet Stones	Blisland	186.131750

Cornwall has only one stone row—

| Nine Maidens | St. Columb | 185.936676 |

STANDING STONES or Menhirs (a selection)

Boswens	St. Just-in-Penwith	189.400329
St. Breock Down (two)	St. Breock	185.969683
Blind Fiddler, The, Trenuggo	Sancreed	189.426281
Karslake	St. Mewan	185.985561
Kerrowe	Zennor	189.453375
Longstone	St. Austell	185.029521
Pipers, The	St. Buryan	189.434248
Tremenheer	St. Keverne	190.778210
Tresvennack	Paul	189.442279

IV

THE BRONZE AGE

THE BEAKER FOLK BROUGHT WITH THEM THE KNOWLEDGE of copper but it was eventually discovered that the addition of a small percentage of tin to copper produced the alloy bronze which is of much greater hardness than that possessed by either of the metals individually. The use of this alloy for making implements in place of stone gives its name to the Bronze Age, which, as the time scale shows, commenced in Cornwall about 1800B.C. Copper at this time was procured from Ireland but Cornwall had tin to mix with it and this fact no doubt brought immigrants to the area. The Bronze Age covers a very long period—1300 years at least—during which changes in people and practices were bound to take place; it is approximately the same length of time from the departure of the Romans from Britain to the present day. To study the Bronze Age means going back at least 3000 years in time—still very remote from today. However, owing to increasing population and the practice of Bronze Age people of burying certain of their dead under large mounds of earth and stones (barrows), monuments are numerous, although not so eye-catching as those of the Megalithic Period. As discovered and examined living-sites are few, it is from barrows that most of the present knowledge of the Bronze Age is derived; it is, therefore, often termed "The Age of the Dead".

BARROWS

Barrows, or tumuli, abound in Cornwall even after centuries of destruction. They may be seen on all sides from the Lizard to Bude, usually sited on high places such as hill-tops, ridges and cliff-tops. Aileen Fox (*South West England* 1965) gives a figure of 850 still in existence as indicated by Ordnance Survey maps, but it is known that there are numbers which are not shown on these so that the total is, in fact, much greater. Although so many must have existed originally, they can bear little relationship to the total population, so it may be that barrow burials were reserved for chieftains or other persons of note.

In the past, such obvious monuments have been attacked with vigour by various people. As far back as the year 1237, King Henry III gave the Earl of Cornwall permission to dig in Cornish barrows for treasure. Miners, in search of stone or the legendary crock of gold, often dug into them. As land became enclosed, farmers, who found barrows a nuisance had no compunction about their reckless removal. H. L. Douch (CAI) quotes from the *West Briton*, 5th February 1819—"A few days since, as the workmen of Mr. Cardell of Tretherras in Lower St. Columb" (St. Columb Minor), "were removing a mound or barrow, in one of his fields, they discovered . . . four urns and a stone coffin . . . Owing to the carelessness of the workmen, three of the urns were broken". From the *West Briton*, 10th August 1821—"Near the top of a cliff . . . in the parish of Lower St. Columb, there are about fifteen of those artificial mounds called barrows . . . Mr. John Cardell, who farms the land . . . determined to remove one of them in order to mix the earth it contained with manure . . . five urns of baked earth were discovered". The account goes on at length describing the variety of objects which were discovered and ends—"We learn with regret that Mr. Cardell proposes to remove the whole of these ancient monuments, in order to clear the ground they occupy for cultivation, and to obtain the earth they contain to mix with manure, and the stone of which the centre is composed, for making hedges". The site referred to is undoubtedly that public, open space still called Barrowfields, in Newquay, on which three barrows still remain, two of which are so reduced as almost to pass un-noticed. Like the *West Briton* of 1821, today's archaeologists deeply regret Mr. Cardell's unsympathetic treatment of ancient monuments.

The last century also produced enthusiastic, well-meaning and, for their time, learned antiquaries who, accompanied by a number of labourers armed with picks and shovels, regularly "opened" barrows. Their method was to dig directly to their centre either from the top or side and many large barrows still show signs of their activities by a hollow on their top. They certainly came across urns and other finds, many of which passed into private collections and have since been lost. Few made any systematic record of their cumbersome work. Fortunately, this predatory approach by farmers and antiquaries is not now possible as most barrows are scheduled as ancient monuments by the Ministry. Those remaining are more likely to be preserved on this account. However, it is occasionally necessary to remove a barrow and when this situation arises, the Ministry mounts an excavation supervised by an experienced archaeologist; as this is a costly process, it is rarely done unless absolutely necessary. During the last twenty years, archaeological excavation has advanced tremendously in its techniques and many weeks are taken in excavating a barrow. Such scientific aids as carbon 14 analysis, which can provide accurate dating, and pollen analysis, which reveals what the natural conditions were when the barrow was built, add greatly to information gained.

Barrow Types

Barrows fall into two types, the 'round' barrow, that is, when viewed from above appears circular, and the 'long barrow' which has an oval or elongated plan. The barrows of Cornwall are round barrows (*plate 9*) although there is one long barrow at Woolley, Morwenstow. The long barrow is of earlier date than the round. Although an isolated one of the latter type is frequently seen, it is more usual to find them in groups or 'cemeteries' up to a dozen or more in number perhaps forming the burial ground of one particular tribe. Careful excavation of round barrows has shown that in construction they fall into set types, the more common being illustrated opposite.

Cornish barrows are usually found to be either of bowl or bell type but an example of a disc barrow may be seen on the top of Brongelly, overlooking Dozmary Pool, St. Neot parish.

Barrow Building

In the Early Bronze Age, inhumation was practiced, the body being placed in a cist (cist=a stone box-like structure) in a crouched position, or on rare occasions, extended. The cist was so built that its covering stone was at ground level. A cairn of stones was built over this followed by layer upon layer of turves and earth. A good example of this type is at Trevelgue, near Newquay, a barrow examined and drawn by W. C. Borlase (NC). In the Middle Bronze Age, when the dead were cremated, the resulting burnt bones were sometimes collected to the centre of the barrow with the remains of the fire, a cairn of stones placed over them and the barrow completed with turves. On other occasions, the cremated material was placed in an earthenware

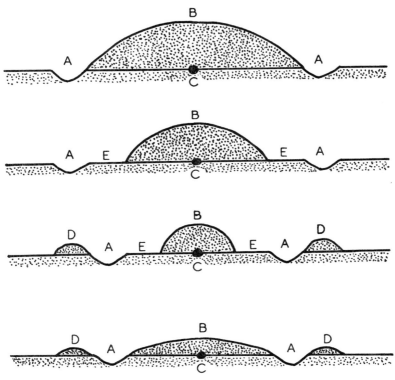

Sections of [top to bottom]: Bowl Barrow, Bell Barrow, Disc Barrow, Saucer Barrow.

A Ditch   B Mound   C Burial   D Bank   E The "Berm"

urn which might stand in the barrow in either an upright or inverted position. In some cases a protecting wall was built around the central cairn; a wooden fence might surround the barrow or in stony areas, a circle of upright stones (=a 'peristalith'), the purpose of both being to retain the structure. A ditch was often dug around the whole, the material excavated in the process being thrown on to the top of the barrow or, as in the saucer and disc types, used to construct a bank around the finished monument. Barrows with peristaliths can be seen on the summits of Trendrine Hill, Zennor, and Alex Tor, St. Breward, as well as at

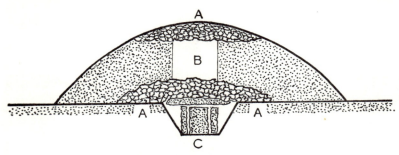

Section of Trevelgue Barrow [after Borlase.]

A Stone cappings   B Layer of clay   C Stone cist containing skeleton and axehead.

Goonzion Downs, St. Neot. These notes on barrow-building are of the simplest and in most general terms; to pursue the subject, specialised books should be consulted, for example, *Ancient Burial Mounds of England* by L. V. Grinsell (1953).

BARROW EXCAVATION

The usual method of excavating a barrow is first to divide it into quarters, or quadrants, each being individually excavated. Between them a part about eighteen inches wide is left untouched, forming a 'baulk'. The purpose of this is to keep before the excavator the original shape of the barrow and from it, measurements can be taken; it also reveals in section, the structure of the barrow. Towards the end of the excavation, the centre is removed and finally the baulks themselves. Plate 11 shows a barrow which has been excavated by this method and its study will make the technique more clear. Barrows were sometimes used more than once. The main, or 'primary' burial, was usually in the centre, any others being made without disturbing this by inserting them towards the edge of the mound. These are known as 'secondary' burials, which might be of members of the same family—just as today a grave is used more than once. Plate 11 also shows this feature.

CREMATION AT A BARROW

The poem "Beowulf", written in the seventh century A.D.
provides a vivid picture of a barrow cremation as it might have
taken place in the Middle Bronze Age. Beowulf, a Swedish hero,
king of the Geats, lying mortally wounded, tells his followers—

> Tell the famed fighters
> To raise on the headland
> A bright barrow over me
> After my burning.
> High on Hronesness
> It shall recall me.
> Sailors shall call it,
> In their distant boats driving
> Over the dark seas,
> Beowulf's Barrow

After his death—

> Then the Geats set ready
> A firm fire-pile for Beowulf,
> And hung it with helmets,
> Shields, and bright corselets
> (As Beowulf had bid them),
> And mourned as they laid him there
> The lord whom they loved.
> And they raised on the headland
> The fiercest of fires,
> The smoke of the wood
> Rising dark from the glow,
> Flames crackling, men keening,
> Till down died the draught,
> And the body was gone,
> Heated through to the heart.
> Then they built up a barrow
> On the edge of the headland
> A high one and wide one
> Far sailors could see,
> And in ten days they finished
> Their great fighter's beacon.
> They had walled round his ashes
> As the wisest advised them,
> They had laid in the barrow
> The rings and adornments of gold.

Standing beside a barrow on a Cornish cliff-top, it is not difficult to imagine such a scene which might well have taken place on that spot 3000 years ago. No doubt, many coastal barrows are used, at least by fishermen, as landmarks. Further, "rings and adornments of gold" have been found in Cornish barrows.

THE EARLY BRONZE AGE

The Early Bronze Age people were an organised society ruled over by chieftains and were workers in metal. They carried on a considerable trade with Ireland on the one hand and the Mediterranean on the other; this was probably in tin, copper and bronze. This is evidenced by objects from these two areas which have been found with their burials, the quantity and quality of which suggests a decidedly wealthy community. They include a wide variety of articles such as pins, daggers, beads, axes and even artifacts of gold. The following are some of the more important finds.

A little over a quarter-of-a-mile north east of "The Hurlers" stands the very large Rillaton barrow—about one hundred feet in diameter. In 1837, a group of miners, said to have been searching in it for 'stone' (which seems unlikely in so stony an area), came upon a cist of granite set in its eastern edge. In the cist were the remains of a human skeleton accompanied by beads, pottery, a spear-head or dagger and a small, ribbed gold cup (JRIC Vol III). The workmanship of the cup, which stands three and a quarter inches high, indicates that it came from the Middle East for similar cups have been found in tombs at Mycenae in Greece. Had it not actually travelled from there, it must have been fashioned by a craftsman who had seen such cups. All the finds from this grave except the cup, have since been lost, but the latter, after being in the custody of the Royal Family for many years, now rests at the British Museum. There is, however, an electro-type copy at the County Museum in Truro (*plate 13*). The grave from which it came is still exposed to view in the side of the barrow.

The finding of a number of segmented, coloured beads in a barrow at Carn Creis, Boscregan, St. Just-in-Penwith, similarly indicate contact with the Middle East for they are of a design known in Crete and Egypt (JRIC Vol. VI). (CM). At Pelynt, of a group of ten barrows, several were excavated in 1854. These provided a number of finds, the most important of which were the remains of a bronze dagger (CM). By its design, it is known that it must have been made in Greece (NC).

When workmen were "levelling ground"—this suggests a barrow—at Harlyn Bay in 1865, they unearthed a flat, bronze axe and two golden crescents of a type well-known in Ireland where many have been found. These are thought to have been used as collars and on account of their shape are known as 'lunulae' or 'lunettes' (CM). They are of fine workmanship and carefully engraved with decoration of the Early Bronze Age (*plate 14*). A third lunula has been found at Hennet, St. Juliot (CM), and a fourth at Gwithian. Like Harlyn Bay, these places are on the north coast in close proximity to Ireland (JRIC Vol. II). Gold being at one time found in that country, it is considered that the lunulae were manufactured there and brought to Cornwall in course of trade. Since no lunulae have been found anywhere else in England, this is an indication of the strong ties between Cornwall and Ireland at that time. The axe found with the lunulae confirms the date of their being placed in the ground for it is of a type unique to the Early Bronze Age (*plate 15a*).

Several barrows have produced miniature daggers with burials. At Harlyn Bay, not far from the finding-place of the lunulae, cliff erosion in 1887 exposed a very fine urn twenty inches in height. With it was a small cup or bowl, a spindle-whorl (q.v.), a bronze pin, a stone implement and a bronze dagger four-and-a-half inches long (JRIC Vol. X). Dagger burials are not common for H. O'Neill Hencken lists only nine in Cornwall (1932); the accidental discovery of yet another in 1964 caused great interest; this took place near Newquay during excavation for a swimming-pool when a fine, inverted urn, the Rosecliston urn, containing cremated bones was disclosed (CA4). With the bones was a bronze dagger three-and-a-quarter inches long (CM). The dagger and the decoration of the urn confirms this to be an early burial. Such small daggers could not have been used as weapons and it is thought they had a ritualistic purpose or perhaps were a treasured possession of the deceased, a symbol of office, or both. Of similar origin are the very small stone axeheads which have been found with early burials. Although occasionally referred to as battle-axes, their length of around four inches would preclude their use in war. A very beautiful example of these was found in one of the two fine barrows on the cliff-edge at Trevelgue, Newquay (*page 34*). In the easternmost of the two lay a skeleton and close to one of its hands, the axe (*plate 2*) (CM). No doubt at the time of the burial, it was complete with a handle of wood and was placed in the hand of the deceased. Others have been found at Harlyn Bay and Ventonvedna, Sithney (CM).

THE MIDDLE BRONZE AGE

The Middle Bronze in Cornwall shows a decline as compared with the previous period, for barrow burials fail to produce much more than the cremated remains of the deceased. Bronze daggers of the Early Bronze Age are absent and no longer are found objects of gold from Ireland or beads from the Mediterranean. In view of the fact that finds of bronze, and even of gold increase in Britain during this period, it would seem that the western sea-going trade gave way to overland routes, Cornwall declining as a result. Metal-working appears to have continued, however, as evidenced by the finding of axehead moulds at Helsbury (q.v.) and a hoard of tin ore at Trevisker (q.v.).

As has been pointed out, during this period cremation of the dead had become the common practice, the remains often being placed in particularly fine earthen ware urns of considerable size— twenty inches or more in height. These urns are curious to Cornwall and appear to have been a local development. The most spectacular are bi-conical in shape, beautifully decorated with a variety of designs made by impressing plaited or twisted cord into the paste of the urn while still soft. A feature of many of them is the fitting of two large, broad handles which have similar decoration to the body of the urn. These handles give the name "ribbon-handled urns" (*plate 16*). There is a display of urns at the County Museum, Truro, and the more inquiring reader should study "Cornish Bronze Age Pottery"—Patchett. Arch. Journ., Vol. CI, 1944— and Vol. CVII, 1952. It should be pointed out that there is in progress some re-consideration of urn styles and nomenclature.

In 1957, at Liskey, Perranporth, the Ministry excavated Crig-a-mennis barrow which proved to be typical of the Middle Bronze Age, its dating being 1300–1350 B.C. (PPS Vol. XXVI. 1960). Although not impressive in size or appearance, which probably accounts for its not having been 'opened' by earlier antiquaries, it presented several features of barrow-building of the period (*plate 11*). At its centre were remains of the funeral pyre and fragments of cremated bone covered by a cairn of stones—the primary burial. Near the perimeter of the barrow were two urns (CM) which also had contained cremated bone—secondary burials. Also revealed were the remains of an encircling wall ("they had walled round his ashes"—Beowulf *see page 35*) and around the whole, a ditch. Finds were meagre and all of stone, apart from a small food-vessel. However, the two fine urns well compensated for the lack of other artifacts. The student who wishes to make further study should read the published reports of the following recent barrow excavations—

The Excavation of Tregulland Barrow. P. Ashbee (PWCF Vol. 1. 4)
The Excavation of the Carvinack Barrow. D. Dudley (JRIC Vol. IV. 4)
The Excavation of the Otterham Barrow. D. Dudley (JRIC Vol. IV. 1)
The Excavation of North Cornish Barrows. C. K. C. Andrew (RTPI Vol. XX)
The Excavation of a Barrow at Glendorgal. D. Dudley (CA No. 1)

During the last two or three decades of scientific barrow excavation, work done has been in the nature of 'rescue' digs only, excavation of sites which are threatened. As these are limited in number, the rites of the Bronze Age people will remain a problem until more work is done.

New weapons came into use during the Middle Bronze Age, the flat axe and small dagger being replaced by the 'palstave'

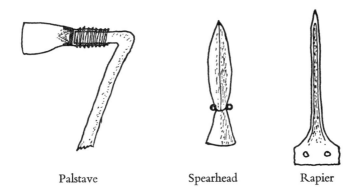

Palstave   Spearhead   Rapier

(*plate 15*), rapier and spearhead. The palstave was an improved

MAP SHOWING SOME OF THE PLACES AND SITES REFERRED TO IN THE TEXT

St. Juliot

Tintagel   Trethevey   Warbstow Bury
       Youlton

Slaughter Bridge

Camelford   Launceston

Lanteglos   Watergate   Lewannick

Rumps Point

Tregear   Rough Tor
mel Estuary   Roscarrock   Fernacre
evone   Helsbury   Garrow Tor   River   Tamar
  Padstow   St. Enodoc   Alex Tor
lyn Bay   St. Kew   Stannon
     Stripple Stones   Bodmin Moor

   Killibury   Dozmary Pool   Stowe's Hill

   Wade bridge   Brongelly   Rillaton   Southill
          Hurlers
Nanscowe   Doniert's Stone   Hingston
visker   Pawton Quoit   Lancarffe   St. Neot   Callington   Down
oggas   Goonzion Downs   Trethevy Quoit
e   Tregear   Bodmin   Cadson
        Castle Canyke   Bury

  St. Columb   Liskeard
  Castle-an-Dinas   Castilly   Lanivet Quoit
       Lostwithiel

  St. Dennis   Hensbarrow   St. Germans

     Castle Dore   Pelynt
      Cunomorus
   St. Austell   Stone   Looe
Resugga Castle   Trewhiddle
     Castle Gotha   Fowey

Caryossa
Golden   Pentewan

Clement
Gare   Caerhayes

Carne
Dingerein Castle

lawes

[Those showing visual remains are underlined]

form of bronze axehead which had a recess on each side to accept a split, wooden haft and a transverse ridge which prevented the head from being driven back into it. Palstaves are on display at the County Museum as well as a rapier found at Illogan plus a spearhead from Gillan.

THE LATE BRONZE AGE

The story of the Late Bronze Age is one of metal rather than barrows. Barrow-building continued but it was of a degraded kind and Aileen Fox goes as far as to suggest that it eventually ended altogether and that burials were made in flat cemeteries—perhaps an influence from the new-comers of the next Age, Iron. Burial urns degenerated to much less elegant styles than the magnificent specimens of the earlier period. They are known as 'Deverel-Rimbury' pots, after two places in Dorset where large numbers have been found. They are straight-sided with a turned-out rim and very little decoration, their almost rectangular shape giving them the name of 'bucket urns'. They have been found in Cornwall at Carn Gloose, Cape Cornwall; Chycarne, and Bosvargus, all in St. Just-in-Penwith; and at Pedngwinion Point, Gunwalloe. Note that all sites are in the extreme west of the county; it might be expected to find them in that area for their makers are thought to have come from the Pyrenees, one section of the people invading south-west Britain at this time.

These people evidently came to Cornwall in search of metal for there is indication of considerable metallurgy taking place—still in west Cornwall. In 1878 a workman "while raising stones for the highway" at Kenidjack Castle, St. Just-in-Penwith, uncovered a large collection of metal materials consisting of axeheads and crude metal. On examination, the disposition of stones suggested that a hut had once stood on the site—perhaps a manufactory. On analysis, the bronze objects were found to contain an unusually high percentage of tin, which is a metal predominant in that area (JRIC Vol. VI). In St. Hilary parish, a similar hoard was discovered comprising axes, swords, spearheads and quantities of broken metal weighing eighty pounds. At Gwinear, in 1880, forty or fifty axes in one collection came to light. It could be argued that all this metal might be of later date but these axes are characteristically late bronze age in design, for these people improved on the palstave by producing the 'socketed celt'—a type of weapon known also in Brittany. The socketed celt (*plate 15c*) is a quite small axehead which, instead of having a depression to take the haft, is hollow at its rear end. The haft is inserted into this and kept in place by a thong running through a small loop cast in the head.

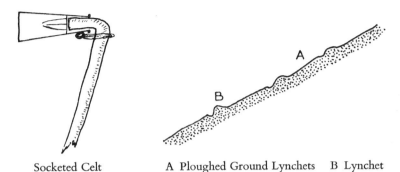

Socketed Celt   A Ploughed Ground Lynchets   B Lynchet

As many celts have been found in Brittany, it has been thought that they came from there to Cornwall but the discovery in 1934 at Helsbury quarry, Michaelstow, of two stone moulds used for casting celts (CM) indicates that some at least were made in the county. As well as the socketed celt, the sword came into use during the Late Bronze Age. This was a heavy, double-edged weapon; several have been found and one from St. Keverne is at the County Museum.

Gold returned to Cornwall in the Late Bronze Age and as in earlier times, it was of Irish origin. Many finds have been made over the years, but two are of outstanding importance. In 1931, under a pre-historic hedge on some croftland at Amalveor farm, Towednack, a gold hoard was discovered. This consisted of two torques, four bracelets and two rods of unworked gold which were clearly the goldsmith's raw material (CM). The pieces were neatly laid together as if hidden deliberately (C. Hawkes—*Man* Vol. XXXIII. 1962). Prior to this the most important gold find had been at Morvah, where six large bracelets (now in the British Museum) came to light. There had been found also one bracelet at Sancreed and a "coil" of gold at the Lizard. It is emphasised again that, apart from the Helsbury moulds, all Late Bronze Age finds are in the extreme west of Cornwall. Tin was available there in plenty and, as has been pointed out, this part of the county lay on the natural shipping route. It would appear, therefore, that there was either a resuscitation of trade in the area or older traditions had lingered on, for all the finds are rich ones, as in the Early Bronze Age.

DOMESTIC SITES

Bronze Age living-sites are rather rare, with the result that knowledge of domestic life is scant. This shortage may be accounted for by the fact that many sites are below present surface level—buried by the natural tendency for the land to rise. Others might have been destroyed by the later Iron Age people who were great builders, or by modern man in search of moor-stone (surface granite). The sites known are situated on some of the wildest parts of Bodmin Moor and on the moors of West Penwith where they are often difficult to see and, to the casual eye, are just a natural, haphazard collection of moorstone. The more experienced eye, however, can often trace the outlines of hut-circles and surrounding walls. The beginner in field archaeology should keep an open eye for large stones standing on edge for they often indicate the work of man, the natural way for a stone to lie being on its broadest surface. Huts often stand amongst small fields which can be distinguished by their 'lynchets'. These were formed by cultivation on sloping ground, owing to the tendency of disturbed soil to move downwards. Thus, the ground at the higher end of each man's plot would, over a period of time, become shallower and the lower end deeper as he ploughed across the slope. This lower side gradually became higher than the upper side of the plot below and a small bank was formed. Such field systems provide evidence of agriculture and may more easily be seen when the sun is low. Excavations at Gwithian revealed the actual plough marks made by these early people in cultivating their land (Thomas–Gwithian, Ten Years' Work WCFC and PWCFC Vol. II, No. 5). Bronze Age sites are particularly noticable on the northern slopes of Rough Tor, near Camelford, especially when conditions are right, that is, when the sun is low and in the Autumn, Winter or Spring months when growth is least.

When Hencken wrote in or about 1930, he was unable to quote an excavated Bronze Age living-site for, at that time, none had been examined; today, the story is different. In 1936 and 1937, the West Cornwall Field Club excavated a settlement, high on the moors, at Trewey-Foage, Zennor, in order to determine its age. The huts stood amongst lyncheted fields with narrow roads running from hut to hut; three of these were excavated, their floor-levels lying twenty-four to thirty inches below present ground level. Finds were few but the excavators were rewarded by finding sherds of pottery which were identified as of a domestic nature and of the Late Bronze Age for the site is dated to 750–500B.C. As Trewey-Foage was the first Bronze Age site to be explored it provided the first domestic pottery of the period to be found in Cornwall (Arch. Journ. Vol. XCVIII. 1941). From 1951–1955, the West Cornwall Field Club excavated the Iron Age village of Bodrifty; this is commented upon in the next chapter. As a result of this excavation, an unexpected feature was revealed, for one of the Iron Age huts appeared to have been built over a much earlier one. The latter produced pottery of the Late Bronze Age, indicating that a settlement of that period existed at Bodrifty prior to the obvious Iron Age site. This might provide evidence already referred to of the later people destroying earlier sites. (Arch. Journ. Vol. CXIII. 1957). A similar circumstance was revealed at Trevisker, St. Eval, when the Ministry excavated a threatened Iron Age camp there in 1955 and 1956. A large hut of this period was uncovered but at a much lower level, and along-side it, a hut of the Bronze Age was discovered, identified by the large amount of pottery of the Late Bronze Age which it produced. In the hut was a considerable amount of tin ore which proves metal-working. Excavation at Gwithian has also produced pottery contemporary with this site. There is evidence that a similar circumstance to Trevisker exists at Kynance Gate, Lizard, where Bronze Age pottery has been found underlying an Iron Age site, but further exploration is needed (PWCFC Vol. II. No. 2).

A site which has been termed "a natural museum" is Garrow Tor, near Brown Willy, in the heart of Bodmin Moor. The gently-sloping ground of the hill must be fertile, for living-sites, dating from the Middle Bronze Age to Mediaeval times, almost cover the hillsides. The pre-historic huts are from ten to thirty feet in diameter. Some stand isolated and others are set in a walled enclosure (pound). They are circular, stone-walled and the larger ones have holes in which were embedded the supports for the roof. Field-work and excavation has shown the inhabitants to have been farmers as well as hunters for traces of their fields are easily seen and querns have been found in the huts. Excavation also produced pottery, beads and slate bangles (Dudley—unpublished).

It may be seen that the Bronze Age, which for many years has been regarded as the age of barrows and metal-working, is coming to life as domestic sites are explored. In retrospect, the age may be seen as one with many intrusions of people from overseas, each bringing distinctive weapons and pottery. During it, metal-workers and merchants, exploiting Cornish tin, brought wealth in the earlier and later centuries. Others brought the practice of cremating the dead, placing the remains in fine urns, burying with them treasured possessions, and building great barrows. It was a time when nomadic life gave way to agriculture and more settled living and, in this way, led to the next period of even greater civilisation, the Iron Age.

BRONZE AGE SITES TO SEE

Barrows

This list is of widely separated barrows, all of which are scheduled ancient monuments, and worth a visit. They are only a few out of the hundreds to be seen. Watch out for others in travelling the county for they are on all sides.

	Parish	Map reference
Allet Common	Kenwyn	190.795485
Bron Gelly (group)	St. Neot	186.195727
Bude, north of (3)	Stratton	174.205074
		174.202081
		174.202089
Bogee Common (7)	St. Columb Major	185.914674
St. Breock Down (many)	St. Breock	185.969683
Barrowfields, Newquay (3)	Newquay	185.821622
Condolden	Tintagel	186.091872
Cubert Common	Cubert	185.781594
Carn Beacon	Veryan	190.913386
Croft Pascoe (many)	Grade-Ruan	190.730200
Carrag-a-Pilez Cliff	Gunwalloe	189.663202
Denzell Downs (6)	St. Mawgan	185.902672
Four Barrows	Kenwyn	190.763483
Hensbarrow	St. Austell	185.997575
Pelynt (group)	Pelynt	186.201544

Pelynt (3)	Pelynt	186.194546
Penadlake (group)	Broadoak (Braddock)	186.142633
Rillaton	Linkinhorne	186.260719
Scotland Corner (many)	St. Breock	185.948681
Tich Barrow	Davidstow	186.147881
Taylor's Cross	Kilkhampton	174.267125
Trevelgue Head (2)	St. Columb Minor	185.825631
Treen Common	Zennor	189.445364
East Pentire (3)	Newquay	185.785614
Whipsiderry (2)	St. Columb Minor	185.834637
Woolley (long)	Morwenstow	174.262166

BARROWS WITH PERISTALITH

Alex Tor	St. Breward	186.118787
Trendrine Hill	Zennor	189.479387
Treslea Downs	Cardinham/Warleggan	186.143685

MISCELLANEOUS (referred to)

Boscregan	St. Just-in-Penwith	189.360297
Gwithian	Gwithian	189.587424 [and area]
Harlyn Bay (finds of lunulae)	St. Merryn	185.872759
Kenidjack Castle	St. Just-in-Penwith	189.354326
Kynance Gate	Landewednack	189.688139
Rough Tor (B.A. site)	St. Breward	186.140815
Trewey-Foage	Zennor	189.464371

V

THE IRON AGE

THE IRON AGE IS SO NAMED BECAUSE IT CONCERNS PEOPLE who had learned the use of iron—a metal which was known on the Continent by 1000B.C.—a date when Britain was still in the Bronze Age. The periods into which it is divided (A, B and C) represent three waves of people . . . "who set out upon a re-markable career of expansion and conquest" (Hencken) and who eventually crossed from the Continent to Britain. They were known to the Romans as Celts and are the people who brought to Brittany, Cornwall and Wales their own particular languages. There are few remains of the Iron Age 'A' group in the South West as far as is at present known, but the 'B' and 'C' are well represented, monuments being both numerous and conspicuous. In the last chapter, it was pointed out that Bronze Age living-sites are not easily visible to the casual eye whereas hundreds of burial places, in the form of barrows, are dotted about the countryside. In the Iron Age, the reverse is true, for living-sites can be seen in plenty, but since these races practised inhumation of the dead in cemeteries, which are now levelled or otherwise concealed, there are no noticable funerary monuments. On this account the Iron Age may be called the "Age of the Living", for most of our knowledge of it is derived from sites occupied by living people. Towards the end of the period, there is the added advantage that written history is available for the first time, giving some insight into the way of life two thousand years ago. Iron Age sites fall under three headings—funerary, defensive and domestic.

FINDS

In the Bronze Age, finds of implements are commonplace, bronze being resistant to corrosion. If iron is left in the soil, particularly the acid, Cornish variety, it rusts and finally dis-integrates, so that tools and weapons of the Iron Age, made of this

48

PLATE 1. *Implements of Flint. A. Microliths B. Leaf Arrowheads C. Early Bronze Age Arrowheads. [By courtesy of The Royal Institution of Cornwall].*

PLATE 2. *Axeheads. A. Paleolithic B. Macehead C. Neolithic D. Beaker Period E. Early Bronze Age Ritual. [By courtesy of The Royal Institution of Cornwall].*

PLATE 3. *The Treveddra (Sennen) Beaker.* [*By courtesy of the Royal Institution of Cornwall*].

PLATE 4. *Trethevy Quoit.*

MEGALITHIC MONUMENTS

PLATE 5. (*Top*) *The Men-an-Tol.*
PLATE 6. *Brane Entrance Grave.*
PLATE 7. (*Bottom*) *Tregeseal Stone Circle.*

PLATE 8. *Standing Stone (menhir) on St. Breock Down.*

PLATE 9. *A typical Cornish round barrow at Carvinack (now excavated and removed).*

PLATE 10. *Carvinack Barrow during excavation. Note large capping of quartz stones in centre and surrounding wall in foreground. Previous 'robbing' is shown by the hollow in the top and the disturbed, dark soil in the centre.*

PLATE 11. *The Crig-a-Mennis Barrow during excavation. A. Baulk B. Central cairn under which were remains of funeral fire C. Part of surrounding wall D. Ditch E. Urn (secondary burial).*

PLATE 12. *Cornish ribbon-handled urns from the Crig-a-Mennis barrow. Between them is a small food-vessel.*

PLATE 13. *The Rillaton Gold Cup (Electrotype copy).* [*By courtesy of the Royal Institution of Cornwall*].

PLATE 14. *Gold Lunulae, or collars.* [*By courtesy of the Royal Institution of Cornwall*].

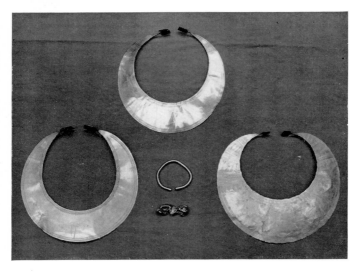

PLATE 15. *Bronze Age Axeheads*
A. *Early (flat)*
B. *Middle (palstave)*
C. *Late (socketed Celt)*
[*By courtesy of The
       Royal Institution of Cornwall*].

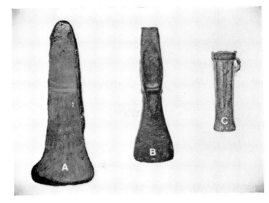

PLATE 16. *The Rosecliston Urn,
a typical bi-conical ribbon-handled urn.*

PLATE 17. *The Youlton Bowl*
[*By courtesy of the Royal Institution
of Cornwall*].

PLATE 18. *Iron Age Pottery. A. Typical Iron Age. B. Glastonbury Ware.* [*By courtesy of The Royal Institution of Cornwall*].

PLATE 19. *A Saddle Quern.* [*By courtesy of The Royal Institution of Cornwall*].

PLATE 20. *The silhouette of Caer Bran, an Iron Age hill fort.*

PLATE 21. *Warbstow Bury, an Iron Age hill fort, showing defensive banks and ditches.*

PLATE 22. *Trevelgue Head, an Iron Age cliff castle, showing defensive ramparts.*

PLATE 23. *Rumps Point, an Iron Age cliff castle. Note the banks and ditches defending the headland.*

PLATE 24. *A Courtyard House at Chysauster.*

PLATE 25. *The Fogou at Boleigh.*

PLATE 26. *The St. Mawes Ingot of Tin. [By courtesy of The Royal Institution of Cornwall].*

PLATE 27. *Roman Milestone at Menheer Farm, Gwennap.*

PLATE 28. *The Roman Villa at Magor during excavation.*
[*By courtesy of the Royal Institution of Cornwall*].

PLATE 29. *The 'Incenvi' Stone in Lewannick churchyard. Note the ogham characters at bottom left.*

PLATE 30. *The estuary at Hayle, arrival point of missionaries from Ireland in the Dark Ages.*

PLATE 33. *The King Doniert Stone,
memorial to a Cornish king.*

PLATE 32. *The Castle Dore
Inscribed stone.*

PLATE 31. *The St. Just Inscribed Stone
with Chi Rho monogram.*

63

PLATE 34. *The remains of St. Piran's Oratory.*

PLATE 35. *The monastic settlement on the Island, Tintagel.*

metal, are rare. However, bronze continued to be used just as it is today and there have been found numerous Iron Age objects of bronze. Most of these are from graves and will be noted under that heading, but mention should be made of a bronze brooch found in a tin-working near St. Austell, dated to between the fourth and second centuries B.C. Also at Pentewan near St. Austell, there came to light a bronze-bound wooden tankard (CM), the style of handle dating it to the Iron Age, and in 1925 came the discovery at Youlton in Treneglos parish, of a fine, hammered bronze bowl (*plate 17*), now known as "The Youlton Bowl" (CM). Of the same period are two bronze necklets from Lelant whilst the excavation at Carloggas, St. Mawgan (q.v.) produced a strip of bronze decoration from a shield (CM).

As there are so many domestic sites to explore, domestic finds are usually numerous. Pottery may be found in great quantities, much of it being finer than that of the bronze age and showing

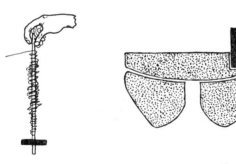

Spindle Whorl in use   Rotary Quern

evidence of having been made on a potter's wheel. Iron Age pottery is of good shape and later specimens, known as "Glaston-bury" ware (*plate 18*) because so much has been found near that Somerset town, is beautifully decorated with scroll-work. A new implement came into use in the Iron Age—the spindle-whorl. These are flat discs about two inches in diameter with a hole drilled in the centre; they are usually of slate or similar stone but metal examples have been found. Spindle-whorls were used in wool-spinning; affixed at the end of a stick, they acted as a weight and at the same time assisted the twisting of the stick between the fingers as the spun wool was wound on to it. Spindle-whorls are

E

still used by primitive tribes. Querns in greater numbers are also found on Iron Age sites. These were used for grinding corn and were introduced in the Bronze Age with the advent of grain-growing. They are of stone, the earlier types being called 'saddle' querns for they are rectangular in shape with a saddle-shaped depression in the upper surface (*plate 19*). Corn was placed in this and by working a smooth stone (the 'muller') to and fro over it, it was reduced to a coarse meal. A later development was the 'rotary' quern, circular and eighteen inches or more in diameter, consisting of two parts rather like modern mill-stones, the top one being rotated by hand. (CM).

BURIAL SITES

Iron Age Cemeteries are discovered only by accident for there is no way of determining their whereabouts. By far the largest and best known of these found so far, came to light in 1900 at Harlyn Bay, near Padstow. When the sandy ground there was being tested with a view to building, a hundred and thirty burials in slate 'coffins' twelve or more feet below ground level were revealed. They were buried to this depth by blown sand. The finds, mostly of stone and bronze, included rings, bracelets, a bangle, a pair of ear-rings, a stone knife and chopper, as well as a wide selection of polished slate implements. Of particular interest was a pair of large bronze brooches of a style common to burials in Spain and Portugal (CM). No weapons were found, perhaps indicating a peaceable folk. There is now a small museum on the site at which many of the finds are displayed whilst a few of the burials have been preserved under glass. (JRIC Vol. 14 and *Harlyn Bay—Bullen*, 1930).

At Trelan Bahow near St. Keverne in 1833, a farmer accidentally discovered a cemetery of several graves, one of which produced a rich assortment of goods (JRIC Vol. 4). These included bronze bracelets, rings, glass beads and a beautifully decorated, bronze hand-mirror, the reflecting surface of which was still brightly polished (BM). This grave was clearly that of a lady and gives evidence of a high standard of living. The mirror, a civilised appurtenance, was of a form which originated in Greece in the fifth century B.C.; like the brooches from Harlyn, it indicated contact with the Mediterranean.

In 1955, coastal erosion exposed a burial at Trevone, near

Padstow. Fragments of several articles were found with the remains of the skeleton, the most important being two brooches, one of bronze and one of iron. The latter was naturally in a poor state, and was decorated with blue glass and red enamel. The bronze brooch is described as "unique" and the iron one as "quite unusual" (CA4). The burial is stated to have taken place about 200B.C.

DEFENSIVE POSITIONS

The Iron Age arrivals in the 'B' period seem to have been somewhat unwelcome, for it was these people who built, between 350B.C. and 150B.C., the fortified encampments which are so plentiful in the county. Adapting natural features of the landscape to their purpose, they built numerous defensive earthworks in strategic positions. Prominent hills and headlands were used, which in themselves would have made retreats without human aid. By building ramparts and ditches, Iron Age man converted them into almost impregnable fortresses. On Ordnance Survey maps in many places on the coast can be seen marked "Cliff Castle", or inland, "Camp". Such sites may be named, for example, "Redcliffe Castle" at Bedruthan Steps, near Newquay; or "Bartine Castle", near St. Just-in-Penwith. Named sites may have a derivation from the Cornish language and in this connection, note should be made of two Cornish words, dynas = a hill fort or earthwork camp, and ker = a fort. Dynas corrupts to 'din', 'dennis' or 'dinas' and ker to 'caer', 'car' or 'gear'. Place-names containing any of these words immediately suggest the presence of an Iron Age fortification, for example, Tregear in St. Kew parish and Dennis Head at the entrance to the Helford river. Mention should be made of the Old English word 'bury' which also means a fortification, as in Warbstow Bury and Cadson Bury. It should be realised that the use of the word 'castle' does not imply a grand, stone building in the Norman style, for some people are very disappointed at not finding such an edifice on a remote Cornish headland.

HILL FORTS

Inland camps fall into two main categories, being built either on an isolated hill-top (for example, Castle-an-Dinas, St. Columb) or on a spur of land in a dominating position (for example,

Warbstow Bury, Warbstow). In the case of hill-tops, once the site had been selected, a series of banks and ditches were built encircling the summit, the innermost bank carrying a wooden palisade. The invader not only had the exhausting task of climbing the hill but was faced with quite formidable defences at the top, with the defenders meantime hurling sling-stones at him from above. It is considered that this form of fortification was developed for use in sling warfare. Spur sites had their banks and ditches constructed across the promontory, some having double defences in order to protect the entrance, for example, Castle Dore, near Fowey or Resugga Castle, St. Stephen-in-Brannel. The siting of

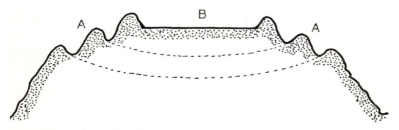

Section of typical Hill Fort.   A Defences   B Living quarters

these fortifications is often of interest and it is instructive to plot them from maps to see how they are situated in relation to the configuration of the land. It may then be possible to consider why they were so placed, for example the succession of camps running along the ancient trackway from the Fowey estuary to that of the Camel. Most of the hill forts are fine monuments and their defences can often be seen from afar as they appear silhouetted against the sky. Special mention may be made of Castle-an-Dinas, St. Columb; Trencrom, Lelant; Castle Canyke, Bodmin; Caer Bran, Sancreed (*plate 20*); Warbstow Bury, Warbstow (*plate 21*); Tregear, St. Kew; and Killibury, Egloshayle. Carn Brea, Redruth, is also a hill of outstanding importance—one which has attracted early man throughout the ages. This fort, of great size, is encircled by defensive banks and on its summit, the huts of Iron Age dwellers are clearly visible. No doubt, ample supplies of tin nearby made this an important site. Chun Castle, Morvah, has thick, stone walls which are said to have stood twelve feet high only a hundred years ago and has a staggered entrance cleverly devised to defeat would-be invaders. Within the circular walls are small huts, a well and a furnace which could have been used for smelting; iron and tin slag was found during an excavation in

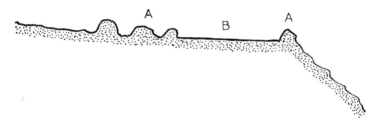

Section of Spur Fort   A Defences   B Living Quarters

1895. Pottery finds date this castle to the first half of the third century B.C. Stowe's Hill, Linkinhorne, is also encircled by tumbled stone walls but it has never been examined; this is a pity, for the whole hill is strewn with pre-historic remains.

Because of their size and lack of threats to their existence, little excavation of hill-forts has been done in recent years. A trial excavation was carried out at Castle-an-Dinas, St. Columb, the finest of all the forts, in 1962 (CA 2) but little was found. Work has also been done at St. Dennis (CA 4) and Castle Gotha (PWCFC Vol. II No. 5 and CA 2). A major excavation took place at Castle Dore in 1936 and 1937 and a very comprehensive report on the work has been published (JRIC Vol. I New Series, Appendix 1951). This splendid camp stands on the ridge-road from Fowey to Padstow; the fact that tin was available nearby might also have influenced its siting. It is circular, its defences consisting of two banks with a ditch between them, the outer bank being extended eastwards to form an additional defence to the main entrance; the earliest settlement here was in the second century B.C. A large amount of pottery was found, much of it the highly decorated Glastonbury ware. There is a further reference to this site in the chapter "The Dark Ages".

CLIFF CASTLES

As a site for a cliff castle, a suitable promontory was selected and a series of banks and ditches constructed across its neck to defend it from the mainland. As the only other approach was by sea and cliffs, such an encampment formed a very strong position. When visited, some may seem disappointing, for not only might the ramparts have become considerably levelled but the sea have taken toll of the headland, thus reducing its size. Others still provide easily recognisable and striking monuments, for example Tre-

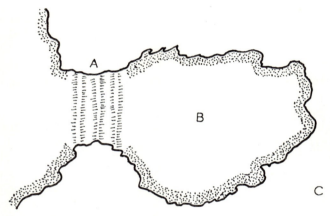

Plan of typical Cliff Castle   A   Defences   B   Living Quarters   C   Sea

velgue Head (Porth Island), Newquay (*plate 22*); Rumps Point, St. Minver (*plate 23*); and Warren Cove, near Treyarnon Bay. The West Cornwall Field Club and its successor the Cornwall Archaeological Society, have examined three cliff castles. In 1939, Maen Castle, Land's End was excavated and it proved to be an early example for it produced the rare 'A' pottery (PWCFC Vol. I. No. 3). In the same year, Gurnard's Head was also dug, this proving to have stepped ramparts built of stone—the reason for this construction no doubt being the fact that the mainland slopes steeply down towards the headland. On the eastern side, what dwellings remained were also excavated (Arch. Journ. XCVII. 1941). In the summers of 1963, 1965 and 1967, a major excavation was carried out at the very fine cliff castle on Rumps Point, St. Minver. The defences were seen to have been built on a very large scale, the outer ditch being thirty-two feet across and fifteen feet deep. The ramparts were stepped similarly to Gurnard's Head and probably for the same reason. Large post-holes in the natural rock of the headland suggest a great wooden entrance gate with perhaps a fighting platform above it. Pottery found in a living-site behind the ramparts suggest that The Rumps was occupied quite late in the Iron Age. An unusual find was a portion of a wooden structure which was carefully removed and examined; as a result, it is considered to be part of a loom—an indication of an advanced form of weaving. (CA 3, 5, 7).

The finest of all Cornish cliff castles, Trevelgue Head near Newquay, was excavated in 1939 but the onset of World War II halted this work and it has never been re-commenced. It is unfortunate also that an account of the work done there has never been officially published, but there is sufficient information available to show what a busy place this site must have been. The headland, which is separated from the mainland by a chasm, was originally defended by six main ramparts, three of these still quite massive (*plate 22*). In passing from the mainland to the island, one passes through them. Even though sea-erosion has taken place, the camp is still of considerable size. Inside the ramparts, two large rooms were uncovered, objects found in them suggesting a date of from 200B.C. onwards. Iron, which occurs in the nearby cliffs, was smelted and the furnace in which this was done was found. Bronze was also smelted in clay crucibles. It is estimated that nearly half-a-ton of metal and slag was present. The kitchen waste-heap (midden) showed remains of cattle, sheep, goats, pigs, birds and shell-fish. The horns of deer were used as implements. The finding of more than twenty spindle-whorls indicates that the women-folk also led a busy life spinning and weaving. Apart from the Iron Age occupation, finds indicated that Trevelgue Head was in-habited by Neolithic and Bronze Age man and later by the Romans. Now, happy holiday-makers are the main users of the Island; it is to be hoped they spare a thought for what lies beneath their feet and for the people who have walked there over a period of 4000 years.

DOMESTIC SITES

On the higher ground in Cornwall, usually open moors, Ordnance Survey maps frequently show "Hut Circles". In more cases than not, these indicate settlements of the Iron Age people who usually lived at about 500 ft. above sea level. Many of these sites are worth visiting, for the remains of the small, round huts are often clearly visible. The best time to see them is during the winter months for in summer they may be concealed by heather and bracken. Watergate, in Advent parish and Mulfra, on the lower slopes of Mulfra Hill in Madron parish, are particularly good sites.

The domestic site of Bodrifty, Madron parish, was excavated by the West Cornwall Field Club from 1951 to 1955 (Arch. Journ. Vol. CXIII). This proved to be a site which was occupied over a very long period, for Bronze Age pottery was found and it was also the first site to produce Iron Age 'A' pottery. The bulk of the pottery—some 3000 sherds in all—was of 'B' date but a little 'C' was also found. The huts, grouped village-wise, were situated amongst primitive fields and surrounded by a protecting wall; their occupants were settled agriculturalists, growing corn and rearing sheep. Although nature has now taken over the site once again and it is, therefore, rather overgrown in summer, Bodrifty should be visited. The whole district teems with the remains of early man for not far distant are the "Beehive Hut", or possible above-ground fogou (q.v.), Mulfra Quoit, the Mulfra hut clusters, Gurnard's Head cliff castle, two stone circles, barrows, passage graves and courtyard houses (q.v.).

Carloggas, St. Mawgan-in-Pydar (note 'car' in the name), which was excavated by the Ministry in 1948 and 1949, proved to be an important site of the later Iron Age. This was in the nature of a rescue dig as the site had been sold for building purposes. The village lay on gently sloping ground leading to the river Menalhyl not far away, from which tin was available. The excavated huts proved to have been built of wood due, no doubt, to the fact that this is a district of woodlands, contrasting with areas like West Penwith, where stone is plentiful and, therefore, the usual building material. Pottery indicated a late dating for much was of Glaston-bury type and some was even of Roman design; sherds of amphorae, large vessels, some three feet in height, used for transporting oils and wines from the Mediterranean were also found—an indication of trade. There were also many finds of bronze brooches and rings, the bronze shield decoration already referred to, querns and spindle-whorls (CM). Quite clearly, this was a highly civilised site for its time and the discovery of Roman ware indicates that some of the Cornish sites continued in being into the Roman period—with which people there was a trade in tin, without doubt. (Arch. Journ. Vol. CXIII).

At present being examined by the Ministry is the settlement of Carn Euny, Sancreed. This has been thought to be a courtyard house site (q.v.) but recent work may well prove it to be similar to Carloggas and the Iron Age phase of Castle Dore. Being in West Penwith, it may prove to be a transitional stage between the usual Iron Age site and the courtyard house culture. (CA Nos. 4, 5, 6, 7).

Goldherring, Sancreed, a site that has been excavated by the Cornwall Archaeological Society in the late 1950's, has also

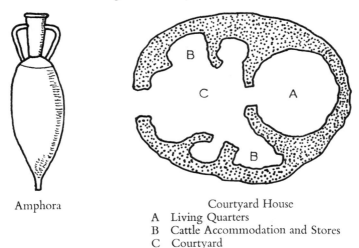

Amphora

Courtyard House
A   Living Quarters
B   Cattle Accommodation and Stores
C   Courtyard

proved to be of later Iron Age date. Two round rooms examined appeared to be of courtyard house type (q.v.). Pottery, which included Glastonbury ware, a fragment of a Roman dish and sherds of amphorae, suggested an occupation from 1–400A.D. Iron slag showed that smelting was carried out; this was found in a furnace and on various parts of the site (CA 8).

COURTYARD HOUSES

Reference has already been made to courtyard houses, a specialised type of dwelling unit known only in West Penwith, which were occupied from first to late fourth century A.D. Each unit consists of a very thick, circular or oval stone wall enclosing an open courtyard. Around this are arranged a round living-room and cattle sheds or storage-places. These self-contained units are usually arranged in groups village-wise. Well over two dozen such sites have now been recognised in the area. The best of these to visit is Chysauster, in Madron parish, which was excavated by the Ministry in 1931, has since been restored and is now open to the public (Arch. 83. 1933). From a study of the site, a very good impression may be gained of its original appearance. (*plate 24*). A second site, Porthmeor in Zennor parish, was excavated from 1933–1935 (JRIC Vol. XXIV. Appendix II. 1937). This had a defensive wall around it, paved ways and an efficient drainage system. Tin and iron occurred and a furnace was revealed. Roman finds were few, suggesting that there was much less contact with the Romans in this part of Cornwall than, for instance, at Carloggas, further up the county. A fine unexcavated site is at Bosullow Trehyllys in Madron.

The people occupying courtyard houses were tinners and farmers; although bearing characteristics of the later Iron Age, they appear to have a place in culture curious to the northern and western parts of the British Isles, for somewhat similar style houses have been found in Wales and Scotland.

Apart from Bodrifty, all the Iron Age sites so far excavated have been late in the period and their occupation continued through Roman times. There is evidence of iron and tin production, of contact with the Romans, as is shown by the finding of Roman pottery, glass etc. but "the contact does not appear to have been closer than might have occurred through occasional visits of Romans as friends, traders, or possibly in some loose supervisory character" (Lt.-Col. F. C. Hurst—Porthmeor report). These are the successors, perhaps, of the people described in the last section of this chapter.

FOGOUS

Occasionally associated with Iron Age living-sites are passages, underground or above ground, called 'fogous'. Their name is derived from the Cornish word 'fogo' or 'fougo' which means a cave or subterranean chamber; similar structures in Ireland are known as 'souterrains'. Fogous are built of dry-stone walling surmounted by large lintels forming the roof (*plate 25*); the latter has disappeared from most of the above-ground examples. Some of them are elaborated by having small chambers leading from the main passage, access to these being by means of a small opening known as a 'creep', for example at Carn Euny, Sancreed, or Boleigh, St. Buryan. Fogous are intriguing structures and they have, on that account, puzzled antiquaries over many years. A variety of suggestions have been put forward as to their purpose, the most acceptable being the one that they were used as storage-places.

IRON AGE CIVILISATION AND TRADE

In considering people who lived two thousand years ago, one is tempted to envisage them as savages, but it must be remembered that the Iron Age races from central Europe came one thousand three hundred years later than those of the Early Bronze Age. One has only to look back that length of time from today to realise what advances can be made in so long a period of human development. The later Iron Age people in Cornwall were settled farmers, tilling the soil and breeding cattle. They worked iron, tin and bronze, made shapely pottery, were spinners of wool and weavers of cloth. It should not be forgotten that at that time, the eastern Mediterranean was in a high state of civilisation and that although Cornwall was far removed from that area, excavation has shown that it was in contact with it through trade. However, there is now no need to rely entirely on this evidence for there are the writings of Greeks and Sicilians to confirm archaeological deductions.

A Greek mariner, Pytheas, c. 330B.C., who claimed to have visited Britain, wrote—"A stormy strait separates the shores of Britain, which the Dumnonii hold, from the Silurian island" (Silures, a tribe dwelling in the east of South Wales). "This people still retain their ancient customs; they refuse to accept coin and insist on barter, preferring to exchange necessities rather than fix prices". This is clear evidence of early trading, also that the inhabitants of Cornwall were not as developed as the Mediterranean peoples where coinage was in circulation. It is also learned from this passage that the south west of Britain had become known as Dumnonia, occupied by the Dumnonii, by which name it was also known by the Romans. Later still, Diodorus, in the first century B.C., gives a more detailed account of trade. "The inhabitants of that part of Britain which is called Belerion" [Land's End] "are very fond of strangers, and from their intercourse with foreign merchants, are civilised in their manner of life. They prepare the tin, working very carefully the earth in which it is produced. The ground is rocky, but it contains earthy veins, the produce of which is ground down, smelted and purified. They beat the metal into masses like astragali and carry it to a certain island lying off Britain called Ictis . . . here then the merchants buy the tin from the natives and carry it over to Gaul, and after travelling over land for about thirty days, they finally bring their loads on horse to the mouth of the Rhone".

This account by Diodorus is accurate and important. He says "the ground is rocky"; the Land's district is certainly that and tin always occurs near granite. The working of "earthy veins" certainly refers to tin-streaming, which means the winning of sur-face tin from soft ground or streams running from it. The "certain island" is considered to be St. Michael's Mount. The "astragalus" of tin dredged from the river at St. Mawes many years ago (*plate 26*) may well be one of those referred to. Tin ingots were so shaped in order conveniently to be slung one on each side of a horse or mule. Archaeology has revealed the homes of the "natives" and has confirmed barter—the Grecian mirror from a grave at St. Keverne and Iberian brooches from Harlyn— treasured possessions from over the seas of a simple, hard-working people who received them in exchange for their tin.

IRON AGE SITES TO SEE

HILL FORTS (a selection)

	Parish	Map reference
Berry Down	St. Neot	186.197689
Castle Canyke	Bodmin	186.086658
Castle Killibury	Egloshayle	186.019736
Castle Dore	St. Sampson	186.103548
Cadson Bury	St. Ive	186.343764
Caer Bran	Sancreed	189.408291
Chun Castle	Morvah	189.405339
Castle-an-Dinas	St. Columb	185.946624
Castle-an-Dinas	Ludgvan	189.485350
Helsbury	Michaelstow	186.084796
Resugga Castle	St. Stephen-in-Brannel	185.940511

Stowe's Pound	Linkinhorne	186.258725
Tregeare Rounds	St. Kew	185.033801
Trencrom	Ludgvan	189.518362
Warbstow Bury	Warbstow	174.201908

CLIFF CASTLES (a selection)

Black Head	St. Austell	186.040479
Griffin's Point	St. Mawgan	185.842665
Gurnard's Head	Zennor	189.432387
Kelsey Head	Cubert	185.765608
Little Dennis	St. Anthony-in-Meneage	190.788256
Maen Castle	Sennen	189.348258
Rumps Point	St. Minver	185.934811
Redcliff Castle	St. Eval	185.849697
Trevelgue Head	St. Columb Minor	185.825631
Treryn Dinas	St. Levan	189.398221
Warren Cove	St. Merryn	185.854736

SETTLEMENTS (a selection)

Bosullow Trehyllys	Madron	189.409342
Bodrifty	Madron	189.445354
Berry Down	St. Neot	186.197689
Carn Euny	Sancreed	189.403288
Chysauster	Madron	189.473350
Goldherring	Sancreed	189.411283
Mulfra	Madron	189.455349
Porthmeor	Zennor	189.434371
Watergate	Advent	186.118813

FOGOUS

"Beehive Hut", Bosporthennis	Zennor	189.438361
*Boleigh	St. Buryan	189.437252
Carn Euny	Sancreed	189.403288
Chysauster	Madron	189.473350
Halliggye	Mawgan-in-Meneage	190.712239
*Pendeen	Pendeen	189.384355
Porthmeor	Zennor	189.434371
Pixies' Hall	Constantine	190.728300

*=in private ground

BURIAL GROUND

| Harlyn Bay | St. Merryn | 185.878753 |

VI

THE ROMAN PERIOD

WHILST CORNWALL WAS PRODUCING TIN FOR EXPORT to the Mediterranean at the time of Christ, revolutionary events were taking place in Britain, for the successful invasion by the Romans in A.D.43 was soon to make great changes in the country. Directed by the Emperor Claudius, the Roman legions landed in south east Britain from whence they pushed northwards and westwards, subduing the natives as they went. Eventually, they built their famous roads and well-planned towns which most have seen or have read about.

The second Roman legion, led by Vespasian, concerns Cornwall the most for this was the one which fought its way towards the south west, storming twenty hill-forts as it went, notably the great Maiden Castle in Dorset. The river Exe was reached and there, on a spur of land, a new tribal capital, Isca Dumnoniorum, was founded (now Exeter). Other troops had moved towards South Wales through Somersetshire and Gloucestershire; as a result, the Dumnonii of west Devon and Cornwall were isolated from the rest of the country. Military invasion was, therefore, unnecessary and life in Cornwall proceeded much as before, whilst the Romanisation of Britain was taking place. Not for Cornwall the fine towns as laid out there; the last chapter has already shown that, apart from the courtyard houses, dwellings were still simple, round huts. In the past, the archaeology of Roman Cornwall has been neglected and knowledge of the period has been limited to chance discoveries or those revealed during the excavation of Iron Age sites. However, there is a new interest arising.

It has often been thought that the Romans did not come into Cornwall to any extent and a glance at a map of Roman Britain will confirm how remote the county was from areas of the new civilisation. They did come though, more perhaps as traders in tin than as conquerors and as has been seen in the previous chapter, there was certainly intercourse between them and the Cornish Dumnonii.

CAMPS

In Cornwall, there are some twenty-four earthworks of typically Roman type, that is, rectangular with rounded corners, contrasting with the circular camps of earlier date. Apart from two, none has been examined and until this is done, their purpose is liable to conjecture. Some are quite small and may have been "marching camps"—quickly thrown up and used only for a brief spell by a few soldiers. Others are on a larger scale and would appear to have been sited strategically, for example, Merthen, which dominates the Helford river. This is a double camp and is about the most rewarding to visit. Golden, in the parish of Probus, is also built on a grand scale, probably to overlook the valley and one-time estuary, below it.

Tregear, at Nanstallon, near Bodmin, has been known to have had Roman connections for a very long time. It was there, early in the last century, that agricultural operations revealed a number of articles of the Roman period. These included Samian pottery (a fine, red ware used by the Romans), coins, a brooch, beads and rings from a horse's bit (Bod. Mus.). In recent years, this not very obvious earthwork, which dominates the valley below, has been systematically excavated. This work shows that it was clearly of a military character and was occupied for a period of from twenty to twenty-five years, early in the first century A.D. (CA Nos. 5, 6, 7). It was probably built to exercise control over the large number of native hill-forts in the neighbourhood but its early abandonment may indicate that the Roman legions were peaceably received.

Carvossa, near Grampound, is also being examined by the Cornwall Archaeological Society. Work has shown that the site contains on its western side a smaller replica of itself. Excavation has so far produced a great variety of pottery, including some Durotrigian. The defensive ditch was itself occupied and the inhabitants were engaged in smelting iron, the great Perran Iron Lode running nearby. Examination of neighbouring fields has showed that the trading settlement soon spilled over the limits of the camp. The evidence of pottery, coins and brooches points to an occupation from 60–120A.D., a similar period as the military station at Tregear. (H. L. Douch—unpublished).

FINDS

Apart from finds associated with Iron Age sites already referred to, most of Cornwall's Roman remains are in the form of coins. However, at a small, apparently domestic Roman site at Bosence, in St. Erth parish, two objects were found in 1756 in a well of some antiquity. One was a tin saucer, with an inscription in Latin and the other a tin jug. These have been identified as belonging to the third or fourth century A.D. No further examination of the site has been carried out. Another find of interest took place "not long before 1821" at Carnanton, St. Mawgan parish. This was an ingot of tin (CM) bearing a Roman stamp showing a helmeted head and the letters DN or DD NN, considered as representing 'dominorum nostrorum'—the tin of our lords the Emperors, that is, a government stamp (VCH). It is interesting that this ingot should be discovered so near the Late Iron Age site at Carloggas, with its Roman finds which have been described in the last chapter; another firm indication of tin trade with the Romans. Lastly, in 1848, a considerable collection of Roman objects was found amongst the sandhills near St. Enodoc, on the Camel estuary. This included coins, Samian pottery, coloured glass beads, brooches, a pair of tweezers and a pink coral necklace. Unfortunately, as so often happened a century or more ago, all the finds passed into private hands and their present whereabouts is unknown. (VCH).

The finding of Roman coins has been recorded since the late eighteenth century. These occur sometimes singly or a few at a time, on other occasions as a large hoard. It is interesting to note that most of the isolated finds consist of coins of the first century A.D., implying that in earlier Roman times there was little coinage in the county; the large hoards usually include coins of the third and fourth centuries, a fact which suggests that circulation of Roman coinage had greatly increased as time passed by. This may be explained by the fact that in the early centuries, the Romans obtained tin from Spain—a source of supply which failed at about A.D.250. It might seem, therefore, that they then commenced to exploit the Cornish metal. About twenty different sites have produced the early coins, amongst them Carn Brea and Trevelgue Head; this makes both these sites of particular note for they display a continuous occupation of at least two thousand years. The hoards of the later centuries produced coins, not in singles, but in thousands—for example, 1600 at Breage, 1000 at Budock, 1000 at Ludgvan and, at Caerhayes, 2500 which were contained in a tin jug. As recently as 1967, over 1000, many of silver, were un-earthed at Gare in Probus parish, as a result of ploughing opera-tions (CM). Such large collections as these might well represent the lifetime's savings of a Cornish tinner.

MILESTONES AND ROADS

To date, five Roman milestones have been discovered in Cornwall. Although so-called, they do not indicate mileage from one place to another, but are monoliths erected on the completion of a road to the honour of the Emperor at the time, whose name they bear. The inscriptions on them are in abbreviated Latin and on that account indecipherable to the casual observer. After the name and site of each stone, a suggested translation is given (VCH).

Tintagel, in the south transept of the parish church.—"To the Emperor Caesar Gaius Valerius Licinius".

Trethevey, approximately mid-way between Tintagel and Boscastle in a private garden.—"To the Emperors Caesars our Lords Gallus and Volusianus".

St. Hilary, in the parish church.—"(erected) in the reign of the Emperor Flavius Valerius Constantinus (Constantine the Great), Pious, Noble Caesar, son of the divine (i.e. dead) Constantius Pius Augustus (i.e. Chlorus)".

Breage, in the parish church.—"To the Emperor Caesar our Lord Marcus Cassianius Latinius Postumus, pious, fortunate, august". This stone is of particular interest since it is now unique. Two other milestones dedicated to Emperor Postumus were known; one in Wales and one at Hadrian's Wall. Both of these have been lost. The Breage stone should, therefore, be carefully guarded.

At Menheer Farm, near Gwennap, in the garden of the farmhouse —"To the Emperor, Caesar, Antonius, Gordianus, pious, fortunate". This stone was discovered as a result of ploughing as recently as 1942. 'Menhir' (corrupted in this instance to 'Menheer'), suggests a standing stone and thus it would appear that, before falling to the ground and becoming buried, this stone stood erect in earlier times, giving the farm the name it has. It is to be wondered if any more such stones have yet to come to light. The reading of the inscription on this stone is from *History of Gwennap*— C. C. James (*plate 27*).

The dating of these stones is important and is as follows:— Tintagel, in view of some doubt as to the correct interpretation of the inscription, is given as "after A.D.250," Trethevey, A.D.251, St. Hilary, A.D.306–308, Breage, A.D.258–268, and Menheer, A.D.238–244, the last named being the earliest so far found. These are dates which coincide with the large hoards of Roman coins and as has already been suggested, it would appear that about A.D.250, the Romans suddenly took greater interest in Cornwall. Their dwindling tin supplies from Spain had to be replaced; to get the metal from Cornwall needed easier communication. Roads were built, but not on the scale as elsewhere in Britain, for there are no obvious remains of them today. Students of the subject suggest that their road from Exeter into Cornwall followed roughly the route of the modern A30 across Bodmin Moor, ending at Redruth. It probably proceeded further, to the important Hayle estuary, but if so the way it went is conjectural. The Menheer, St. Hilary, and Breage stones imply a road running in the hinterland of Mount's Bay; it has been suggested that the Romans used both Porthleven and Loe Pool (the latter in their day an open estuary) as ports. The Tintagel and Trethevey stones suggest a road in north Cornwall. This is possible, for there was the obviously important Iron Age site at Rumps Point and not far beyond it, the Camel estuary, so important as a harbour. Not far from Rumps Point, the entirely un-Cornish place-name of Plain Street, has a decidedly Roman flavour. Today, one house stands there but Roman legions might have passed that way long ago.

LIVING-SITES

The most interesting archaeological discovery of recent years took place at Magor farm, near Camborne, in 1931. Ploughing operations there uncovered some tessellated pavement which, on being examined by experts, was pronounced to be of Roman origin. Such a find implied the presence of a dwelling and an excavation took place, disclosing the remains of a Roman villa of a type common in the Roman province of Britain, but hitherto unknown in Cornwall. It is interesting to note that the Cornish word 'magor' means an ancient ruin; it might well be that when the farm was named, the villa was visible in a ruinous condition. Such villas are rectangular in shape (contrasting with all dwellings so far met with which have been circular), with a central, paved corridor with rooms leading from it, and a wing at each end (*plate 28*). Some of the walls had on them coloured, decorated plaster two-and-a-half inches thick. Twelve Roman coins, in mint condition, were found in a wall-recess and several others in different parts of the building. Pottery was surprisingly scarce, but amongst that found were sherds of amphora ware and other typical Roman vessels. Bronze objects were also few; they included a brooch and an enamelled stud. An unusual find was a great quantity of iron nails, square in section and with round heads. As many of them were found piercing slates it can be assumed that they came from the roof. The exact role which this house plays in the history of Roman Cornwall is not clear. It was first occupied at about A.D.150 and eventually abandoned at A.D.230–240— a period before the Romans were directing their attention to Cornish tin. Certain crudities of construction and lack of amenities suggests that it was not built by a Roman at all but possibly by a local person who had seen such villas outside Cornwall and had attempted to copy them on his return home. (JRIC Vol. 24. Supplement 1934).

Only one other site has provided domestic associations and this is at Gwithian, three miles west of Magor. Excavations there in 1956 disclosed a native site which produced Samian ware and other pottery of the first to third centuries A.D. It is suggested that there were connections between the two sites but exactly what they were is doubtful (WCFC "Gwithian—Ten Years Work").

Much work has yet to be done towards the elucidation of Cornwall in Roman times. The picture so far presented suggests that there was little change in the mode of life and that in this remote corner of the Empire, Roman influence was slight. It would seem, though, that there was eventually penetration into the county in search of tin, in return for which the Cornish Dumnonii were paid either in cash or kind.

ROMAN PERIOD SITES TO SEE

EARTHWORKS (Camps)
These are usually disappointing, not being built on the grand scale of the Iron Age nor in such inaccessible positions. Cultivation has often reduced them wholly or in part to invisibility.

Name (a selection)	Parish	Map reference
Bosence	St. Erth	189.575325
Carvossa	Probus	190.919483
Golden	Probus	190.924469
Goonzion	St. Neot	186.171677
Grambla	Wendron	189.693283
Merthen (double camp)	Constantine	190.731266
Tregear, Nanstallon	Bodmin	186.034670

DOMESTIC

Gwithian	Gwithian	189.581428
Magor, site of	Illogan	189.637425

MILESTONES

Breage, in church	Breage	189.618285
St. Hilary, in church	St. Hilary	189.551313
*Menheer Farm	Gwennap	190.719421
Tintagel, in church	Tintagel	185.051885
*Trethevey	Tintagel	185.076892

[*=in private ground]

VII

THE DARK AGES

THREE HUNDRED AND FIFTY YEARS IN HISTORY, AS opposed to pre-history, is a long time during which much can happen; one has only to look back this length of time from the present day to realise how conditions can change. By A.D.400 the people of Britain regarded themselves as Romans and were leading settled and well-regulated lives, Cornwall being very much an outpost of this society. "To the people of Britain in the first fifty years of the fourth century A.D., prosperous years of peace, Roman civilisation must have seemed almost as permanent and unshakeable as did our own in the Spring of 1914", as Dr. Hencken aptly summarises the situation.

However, the Romans were being troubled by Germanic and other tribes who were plundering their territories on the Continent and by the year A.D.400 these attacks had become serious. As a result, they were obliged gradually to withdraw their legions from the remote province of Britain, with its long lines of communication, so that they might better defend their Continental possessions. As the situation became increasingly desperate, in the year 410A.D., Emperor Honorious addressed a letter to the towns of Britain informing them that they must thereafter look to their own defence and Roman withdrawal became complete. So ended the Roman occupation of this country.

The fact that Honorious instructed the Romano-British people to attend their own defence suggests that Britain had been attacked in the past or was liable to be in the future. Its rich lands had long been coveted by overseas tribes other than the Romans; the movement of peoples from the Continent to Britain in prehistoric times has already been noted. Removal of the Roman legions provided an opportunity for invasion in the East by Angles, Saxons, Jutes and Danes from countries now known as the Netherlands, West Germany and Denmark. As far as Cornwall is concerned, the Saxons are of the greatest importance historically.

85

They established the states of East, Middle and South Saxons (Essex, Middlesex and Sussex) and moved westwards to form Wessex (West Saxons), eventually dominating what may now be called England (after the Angles). The early Saxons were not only heathen but illiterate, with the result that there is little written record of these quarrelsome days. Because of this, the period from the fifth century almost until the coming of the Normans in 1066, is known as the Dark Ages when "a twilight descends upon Britain almost as intense as the pre-historic night which enveloped it before the coming of the Romans". (Hencken). This, however, was written forty years ago and it is doubtful if the writer would express the same thought today for, since then, much more has been learned of the Dark Ages in Cornwall so that the 'Twilight' is not quite so 'intense' as it was then.

THE IRISH AND WELSH INVASION

Whilst revolutionary events were taking place in England, it should not be forgotten that by reason of its remoteness, Cornwall, like Scotland and Wales, remained Celtic still. Christianity prospered and shadowy figures of kings and saints played their part in its history. Nevertheless, like the east coast, the county was not free from invasion and in view of its geographical position, this came from Ireland and Wales, with which countries there had always been close connections. Some of the invaders might have come as plunderers, others on entirely peaceful missions. Immigrants from these parts naturally approached Cornwall via the north coast where there are the broad estuaries of the rivers Camel and Hayle. These provided not only a safe landing-place but easy access to the interior of the county also. It is considered that the invasion by these people took place approximately A.D.450 to 550 and of those who crossed to Cornwall the evangelising holy-men and women, popularly called 'saints', are the most interesting. They are the people who have left behind as their memorial Cornwall's many saintly place-names—St. Columb, St. Ives, St. Mawgan, St. Tudy, St. Mabyn and a host of others.

In view of the fact that during the Dark Ages recorded history is scant, it may seem paradoxial that much knowledge comes from written words—words "not to be read in the library but in the field" (Balchin). They are writings, often in poor lettering with mis-spellings, which are to be found on memorial stones.

Together with recorded 'lives' of the saints, they give an insight
into some of the events taking place about A.D.500 and confirm
the Irish/Welsh invasion. "It is with these battered scrivings that
the archaeological records of Christian Cornwall begin"
(Hencken).

The Irish brought with them a form of shorthand which is used
for inscribing on stone—the ogham script—in which normal
letters are indicated by strokes along or across a line as follows

Its place of origin is not known for certain but is considered to be
Ireland since no less than 315 ogham inscriptions are known there,
as compared with 48 in England and Wales. Cornwall has six,
more than any county except Pembrokeshire and Carmarthenshire
—both areas in greater proximity to Ireland than Cornwall. It is
indicative of Irish entry via the Camel that five of the six Cornish
ogham stones are found in the area of that river. They all carry an
inscription in Latin, the oghams repeating the name of the
commemorated person. These are, with inscription,

In St. Kew parish church. "Iusti".—Justus. The stone being only
a fragment, no more appears.

Near Roscarrock, St. Endelion. "Brocagni hic iacit Nadotti filius".
—Brocagnus lies here the son of Nadottus.

Slaughter Bridge, Minster. "Latini ic iacit filius Macari". Latinus
lies here the son of Macarus. This stone is known as King
Arthur's Tomb.

Lewannick, in the parish churchyard. "Incenvi memoria".—
To the memory of Incenvus. (*Plate 29*).

Lewannick, in the parish church. "(Hi)c iacit Ulcagni".—Here
lies Ulcagnus.

The sixth ogham stone is in the churchyard of the parish church
of St. Clement, near Truro. "Ignioc—Vitali fili Torrici".—Ignioc
—Vitalus son of Torricus. It has been suggested that the appearance
of the name Ignioc is due to a second use of the stone. This stone
may appear a long way from the river Camel but standing on an

estuary as it does, it may well lie at the southern end of a trackway from the Camel to the Fal.

Two further stones in the Camel area are of interest. Although having no oghams, the names they carry are Irish.

At Lancarffe, Bodmin. "Dunocati hic iacit fili Mercagni".—
  Dunocatus lies here the son of Mercagnus.

At Nanscowe farm, St. Breock. "Ulcagni fili Severi".—Ulcagnus son of Severus. (Note that Ulcagnus also appears at Lewannick).

The Roscarrock stone is of particular interest for it carries the name of Brocagnus which can be identified with Brychan of Wales who had Irish connections. Brychan raised a family of twelve sons and twelve daughters, all of whom are reputed to have become saints. In the right-hand panel of the Young Womens' window at St. Neot parish church, famous for its stained glass windows, Brychan is depicted. He has in his lap a napkin containing the faces of a few of his numerous children. It would be reasonable to guess that out of so large a family of saints, some would come to Cornwall; in fact they did, for there are a number of parish churches mainly in the north of the county dedicated to the children of Brychan, amongst them St. Ive, St. Endellion, St. Minver, St. Teath, St. Mabyn, St. Kew, St. Issey.

Early Christianity

In the West, the Hayle estuary (*plate 30*) provides further evidence of Irish influence and early Christianity. Standing at Bleu Bridge, Gulval, near the ancient trackway from Hayle to St. Michael's Mount, is a stone bearing an Irish name reading "Quentauci ic Dinui fillius".—Quentaucus here son of Dinuus. At Carnsew, overlooking the estuary, an inscribed stone was found in 1843, lying alongside a grave. This is now set in a wall at a public open space near its finding-place. Its inscription has proved controversial since it is worn almost to extinction in places. The usually accepted version is "Hic in tumulo requievit . . . Cunaide (or Cenui) hic (in) tumulo iacit. Vixit annos XXXIII".—Here in the grave fell asleep . . . Cunaide (or Cenui) lies here in the grave. Lived 33 years. Professor Charles Thomas has explored the inscription at length (OC Vol. I No. 3) and concludes that it "is clearly Christian and early fifth century" (PWCFC Vol. II No. 2), making it as early a gravestone one is likely to see.

Remote Christianity in Cornwall is also indicated by stones bearing one of the earliest of Christian symbols—the Chi Rho monogram. This is derived from the first two letters of the Greek word for Christ and most commonly appears as a letter 'P' with

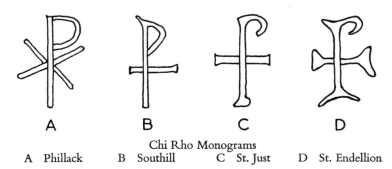

A Phillack   B Southill   C St. Just   D St. Endellion

Chi Rho Monograms

A Phillack   B Southill   C St. Just   D St. Endellion

an 'X' superimposed on its stem. There are, however, variations. Three of these have been found in west Cornwall at Phillack, where it is to be seen high on the south porch of the parish church. Dated about A.D.450.

St. Just-in-Penwith, now in the parish church (*plate 31*). This stone also has the inscription 'Selus ic iacit" — Selus lies here. Dated first half of the fifth century.

St. Helen's Chapel, Cape Cornwall. Unfortunately, this stone is now lost.

The Brocagnus stone, St. Endellion, (page 87) also has a Chi Rho and yet another may be seen in the churchyard at Southill parish church.

As in the case of the Camel estuary, it is accepted that Irish saints landed at Hayle. About 1540, John Leland wrote "Breaca came to Cornwall with a party of many saints". The parish church of Breage is dedicated to St. Breaca; in addition there are many other church dedications to Irish saints in the vicinity of the Hayle estuary. The better-known of these are St. Ives, Lelant, Redruth, Crowan, Gwithian, St. Erth, Phillack, Sithney and Gwinear.

Archaeological excavation has provided yet more evidence of contact between Cornwall and Ireland. In several sandy areas of the north coast, notably at Gwithian, a distinctive type of pottery, dated to the sixth century A.D., has been found. This has been named "grass-marked" pottery since the bases of vessels show the impression of chopped grass upon which they were placed whilst the clay was still soft—a means of preventing sticking. Investigation has shown the only other location for this type of pottery to be north-eastern Ireland. This is where St. Breaca is said to have been born; it is probable that her followers brought with them this idea in pottery-making. (WCFC "Gwithian— Ten Year's Work").

CORNISH KINGS

That kings existed in Cornwall during the Dark Ages is generally accepted but the more enquiring mind may wonder if these are merely legendary for a central figure ruling the whole of the county as it is known today is implied. This was not so but without doubt there were local chieftains holding sway over certain areas. Much information comes from early chronicles but it is beyond the intention of this volume to examine these. (The Early Kings of Cornwall. CR Winter 1969). There are, however, three monuments to visit which indicate the existence of so-called kings.

High on the moors of West Penwith is a stone which is marked on the Ordnance Survey map as "Men Scryfa"—the written stone. The walk to reach it is a pleasant one, in the course of which the Men-an-Tol is passed (*page 25*). The Men Scryfa is dated to the early sixth century, its inscription reading "Rialobrani Cunovali fili"—Rialobran son of Cunoval. These names mean respectively 'Royal Raven' and 'worthy fame' and would appear to commemorate a chieftain and his son who might have ruled over West Penwith.

The name of a chieftain, Gereint, appears in the Anglo-Saxon Chronicle A.D.710 where he is referred to as "king of the Britons". His name is popularly connected with the Roseland district of Cornwall. In the parish of Gerrans are the remains of an earthwork called Dingerein Castle (Dingerein=Gereint's castle). Furthermore, the dedication of the parish church to St. Gerendus also suggests his association with the district. Scholars now regard this as entirely fictitious. The legend is that Gereint is buried in the great barrow at Carne, Veryan, but this can certainly be dismissed for it is hoped that readers of this book will now realise that barrows were built long before this period.

A stone, with an inscription which has provoked much speculation, stands at a road junction a mile or so from Fowey towards Par, near the disused entrance to Menabilly House. This stone is variously termed the 'Castle Dore' stone, the 'Cunomorus Stone' and the 'Tristran Stone' (*Plate 32*). It is dated to the mid-sixth century. Much of the inscription is still quite clear but the first word has been variously read by different experts. The now accepted reading is "Drustaus (or Drustanus) hic iacit Cunomori filius"—Here lies Drustaus (or Drustanus) son of Cunomorus. Drustaus has been equated with Tristran and Cunomorus with Marcus or Mark so that the final reading is considered to be Tristran, son of Mark, lies here. (JRIC Vol. 1 New Series. Appendix 1951). The latter is a known historical figure of the sixth century and many will know the love story of Tristran and Iseult.

One-and-a-half miles from the Cunomorus stone, alongside the road to Lostwithiel, is the earthwork Castle Dore. It is there that the stone was found—hence one of its names. Castle Dore has already been referred to as an Iron Age camp (*Page 69*). An excavation carried out in 1936 proved this to be the case and further, that it had been deserted for over three centuries throughout the Roman period. Post-holes were found indicating that, probably in the sixth century, a wooden palace had been built within the older defences. At such a period as this, such a building could only have been occupied by a person of substance and its discovery gives added weight to the belief that one King Mark ruled over this part of Cornwall.

Another figure referred to in the Anglo-Saxon Chronicle is commemorated on "King Doniert's Stone" in the parish of St. Cleer north of Liskeard. This monument stands beside the road between Redgate and Minions, protected by a surrounding wall (*plate 33*). The inscription, which is very clear, reads "Doniert Rogavit pro Anima"—Doniert ordered (this to be set up) for (the good of) his soul. Doniert can be identified with Dumgarth, a Cornish king or chieftain who was accidentally drowned in A.D.878—the lettering and ornament of the stone agreeing with this date.

Doniert is reputed to have been the last of the Cornish kings for the Saxons had already defeated the Cornish in the east by A.D.838. In the extreme west, however, there is evidence that there was at least one who ruled at a later date. There is a cross standing outside

Penlee House in Penzance, which at one time stood in the market-place. Although it has a more ancient appearance, it is dated to the tenth century A.D. On its reverse, at the bottom left-hand corner, is the inscription "Regis Ricati Crux"—the cross of King Ricatus. Beyond the validity of the name, nothing is known of Ricatus but in spite of the Saxon success in the east of the county, he could well have ruled after Dumgarth since he was in the far west which the Saxons had not yet reached.

It may well be asked at this juncture why no mention has been made of King Arthur. This is a reasonable question for, on studying a map, the reader might see marked on Bodmin Moor "King Arthur's Hall", "King Arthur's Bed" or "King Arthur's Downs"; or might have heard of "King Arthur's Tomb" or perhaps the legend that it was into Dozmary Pool that the sword Excalibur was thrown. If he has been to Tintagel, where even the Norman castle on the cliffs is marked on the map as "King Arthur's Castle", he has been overwhelmed by King Arthur. No reference to this noble king-warrior has been made, for there is no historical evidence whatever that he had any associations with Cornwall.

THE CHURCH

During the Dark Ages, the church developed entirely as a monastic institution. It is likely that on arrival in Cornwall, the missionaries from Ireland and Wales sought a convenient piece of land on which to settle, building around it a fence or wall. Within, a humble oratory was constructed, at first perhaps of wood and later of stone. One of these early oratories may still be seen in the midst of the great sand-waste of Gear and Penhale Sands, near Perranporth. This is the oratory of St. Piran (*plate 34*) who was of Irish origin; it is right, therefore, that his holy cell should be found on the north coast. A very small building, "The Lost Church", has been preserved by being buried in blown sand for centuries. Early in the last century, a gable-end was noticed protruding from the sand and in 1910 this was excavated and the present protective shell placed over it. In modern times it has suffered from flooding and vandalism, but what is seen there does give an insight into what these early holy buildings would have looked like. It is not as old as one would wish it to be, for it is considered to be no earlier than the eighth century. Never-the-less

this could well be the earliest Christian building in the country.
There is a further simple chapel at Gwithian, that of St. Gothian, which is similarly overwhelmed by sand. This is not visible today, but early in the last century was sufficiently uncovered to enable a plan of it to be drawn. This shows that it is larger than St. Piran's and slightly more developed in style, making its dating tenth century but there might have been a smaller, earlier building on the site.

After death, the body of the saint would have been buried within the enclosure, thus sanctifying it and giving it his or her name. It then became holy ground. As time progressed, a larger building was raised (as suggested at St. Gothian's), this being followed by a larger still, ending today with a parish church. This may still be dedicated to the original Celtic saint. This development may well account for the remote places in which some Cornish parish churches are found. Of particular interest are those sited on the river estuaries which have been the main entrances to the county by sea for thousands of years. Examples are St. Winnow, St. Enodoc, Ruan Lanihorne, Lelant, Phillack, Mylor, St. Just-in-Roseland. Allowing for silting of estuaries and creeks, even some of those which appear to be inland today, must have been estuary churches at one time—Creed, Helston, Lostwithiel, St. Erth. Not all sites eventually produced a parish church, however. Many have simply disappeared but their original whereabouts can often be identified by place-names for there is a Cornish word 'lan' which implies a monastic enclosure. This has become a prefix in such names as Laneast, Lanhydrock, Lanivet, and many smaller, lesser-known places.

There also developed monastic sites comparable with those of Wales, but not on the same large scale. One of these, Tintagel, has been examined by archaeological excavation (*plate 35*). Most people go to Tintagel to see the castle on the cliffs or, rightly, to imbibe the coastal magic of this place which is so full of legend and genuine history. On "The Island" are the remains of a monastic site preserved by the Ministry. These can be seen on its top and north-eastern slopes. The monks who occupied it, between twenty and a hundred in number, probably crossed to Cornwall from Wales with other early immigrants for the original site "cannot be much later than A.D.500" (JRIC Vol. 25. Appendix 1942). Amongst pottery finds were sherds of amphorae and other fine wares, the origin of which can be traced to the eastern Mediterranean. This fact gives an indication of much wider sea-going trade at this time than the comparatively local contact with Wales and Ireland.

A find made in 1774 at Trewhiddle, near St. Austell, indicates a certain amount of wealth in the Celtic church. This was a hoard of silver articles, carefully hidden by a priest or monk who was never able to retrieve it. It comprised mounts for drinking-horns, rings, a brooch, a large pin with an engraved head, a small box, a scourge of silver wire and other engraved objects. There were also a number of Saxon coins, many of silver, and a silver chalice. The coins suggest that this treasure was buried about A.D. 875 this dating making the chalice the oldest piece of church plate in existence. It is now in the British Museum but an exact copy is displayed at the County Museum, Truro.

DOMESTIC

Until recent years, Dark Age domestic sites were not known. A small one was uncovered at Gwithian c. 1950 (WCFC—"Gwithian, Ten Years' Work"), but an accidental discovery in 1934 at Mawgan Porth, near Newquay, led to a major excavation there by the Ministry 1950–54. This revealed three groups of buildings, rectangular in shape and arranged around a courtyard. They were situated on the bank of a tidal creek which once lay behind the present beach. The main dwelling-house of each group was a long, narrow room which housed both animals and human beings—cattle at one end, people at the other. The occupants led a quiet, pastoral life and bone remains showed that they kept oxen, sheep, horses, dogs and cats. Their food was cooked in earthenware vessels which had two large lips with a bar inside them by means of which the pot was hung over a fire. The lip prevented damage to the supporting thongs by the fire. This type of pottery is known as 'bar-lip' or 'bar-lug' and has been found at several sites in Cornwall of this period. It occurs at a few sites in eastern England but apart from these, is mainly found on the Continent between the Rhine and Denmark on the coast. Although this Cornish pottery was locally made, it is suggested that the original idea for this type of pot came from there, brought by Fresian traders. The most important find at Mawgan Porth was a silver coin of Ethelred II, minted at Lydford in Devon, and of the date A.D.990–995. This gives an accurate dating for the settlement which is of the utmost importance since it gives an insight into life at the end of the Dark Ages. (R. L. S. Bruce-Mitford—*Recent Archaeological Excavations in Britain*, 1956).

THE SAXONS

Whilst remote Cornwall had been experiencing the life of a quiet back-water, major events had been taking place in Britain. The Saxons, now Christianised by St. Augustine and his followers who landed in Kent in A.D.597, had conquered the country apart from the fringe areas of Scotland, Wales and the extreme south-west. The peoples of these areas now became known as the 'British' as opposed to the English in the rest of the country. By A.D. 700 the West Saxons were established at Taunton and Exeter, thus severing the British of Devon and Cornwall from their compatriots in Wales. The final defeat of the last remnants of the Dumnonii was in sight. From Exeter, the Saxons advanced westwards towards Cornwall along the north side of Dartmoor. A glance at a map will show this to be quite a natural manoeuvre; the obstacles of the high land and the river Tamar were avoided. The British were pushed westwards "to the very coast of the Atlantic, into what is now north-east Cornwall". (Hoskins— *The Westward Expansion of Wessex*, 1960). The coast would have been the stretch from Hartland Point almost to Boscastle and the boundary would have been the river Ottery. A further advance to the Camel in A.D. 721 or 722 resulted in a defeat of the Saxons there by the Cornish—or the 'West Welsh' as the Saxons had named them in contrast to the Welsh of Wales. It is evident that considerable resistance to the Saxon advance was in being. Saxon influence in north-west Devon and north-east Cornwall is still evidenced by the number of place-names with the suffixes of 'stow', 'ton', 'worthy' and 'stock' (Poundstock, Morwenstow, Stratton, Holsworthy, etc.). It is not surprising that in north Cornwall there should be a stone with an inscription, not in Latin (a language soon to be relegated to the church), but in the English of the time. This stands on the south side of the parish church of Lanteglos-by-Camelford and reads "AElseth 7 Genereth wohte thisne sybstel for AElwines soul 7 for heysel".—Aelseth and Genereth made this monument for the soul of AElwine and for themselves.

Resistance to the Saxons continued. In A.D.825, the West Welsh fought a battle against them which took place well into Devon and in A.D.838, they even enlisted the help of the Danes, who had by this time reached the west on marauding raids. The combined forces met the Saxons at Hingston Down, near Callington, but the outcome was a final defeat. It was not until a hundred years later, however, that Athelstan completed the conquest by subjugating the extreme west of the county. Thus, Cornwall came under the domination of England for the first time. The victors gave large parcels of land to the Bishop of Sherborne and brought new ideas in government. The River Tamar was designated the boundary between Cornwall and Devon and the county was divided into areas called 'hundreds' as had been done in England. The parochial system was introduced into the church and a diocese of Cornwall was created in A.D.931 with bishop Conan, seated at St. Germans, at its head. The county was named 'Cornewalas' (whence it gets its modern name), which comes from the Saxon word 'wealos' which means 'strangers', that is, different people, which the inhabitants were. This fact, combined with a study of the landscape, enabled Professor W. G. V. Balchin to write of Cornwall in 1954, a thousand years after the Saxon conquest, "although of England it is quite un-English".

DARK AGES SITES TO SEE

INSCRIBED STONES

	Parish	Map reference
Bleu Bridge	Gulval	189.478318
Carnsew	Hayle	189.557371
Castle Dore	Fowey	186.110524
St. Just, Chi Rho	St. Just-in-Penwith	189.372314
St. Kew, church	St. Kew	186.021769
Lancarffe	Bodmin	186.082689
Lanteglos, church	Lanteglos-by-Camelford	186.088823
Lewannick, church	Lewannick	186.276807
Men Scryfa	Madron	189.427353
Nanscowe	St. Breock	185.969708
Penlee House	Penzance	189. town
Phillack	Phillack	189.565384
Redgate, 'Doniert'	St. Cleer	186.236688

Roscarrock, 'Brocagnus'	St. Endellion	185.990797
Southill, church	Southill	186.330726
Slaughter Bridge	Minster	185.109857

MISCELLANEOUS

Castle Dore	St. Sampson	186.103548
Dingerein Castle	Gerrans	190.882376
St. Germans church	St. Germans	186.359577
St. Gothian's Chapel (site of)	Gwithian	189.589418
St. Helen's Chapel	St. Just-in-Penwith	189.353319
Hingston Down	Callington	186.390711
Mawgan Porth settlement	St. Mawgan	185.851673
St. Neot, church	St. Neot	186.186678
St. Piran's Oratory	Perranzabuloe	185.766563
Tintagel, Island	Tintagel	185.050891

EPILOGUE

In his book *The Cornish Riviera*, published in 1929, S. P. B. Mais wrote:

". . . in the Duchy medievalism still exists, the candle lit by the early saints still burns, the age of chivalry is emphatically not dead, and our remote ancestors still haunt the ancient places".

Forty years later one wonders if medievalism still exists; immigration, now coming from the East, may have changed this. It is certain that the 'candle' still burns, its flame re-kindled by John Wesley two hundred years ago. That chivalry is not dead is discovered when enlisting help from the true Cornish people who are so friendly and helpful to those in need. Perhaps they are the descendants of those Iron Age folk who were "very fond of strangers and civilised in their manner of life". Most certainly "our remote ancestors still haunt the ancient places" for it is possible to stand in parts of Cornwall and feel the mystery of the past—to feel an indescribable presence—and that one is existing in times very remote from our own. If this book enables the reader to experience this even to only a small degree, or at least arouses an interest in the Cornwall which is to be cherished, then it will have achieved to some extent its writer's purpose.

BOOKS FOR FURTHER READING
OR FOR REFERENCE

Cornwall—The Making of the English Landscape Series	W. G. V. Balchin	Hodder & Stoughton
South West England	Aileen Fox	Thames & Hudson
The Archaeology of Cornwall and Scilly	H. O'Neill Hencken	Methuen
Teach Yourself Archaeology	S. G. Brade-Birks	English University Press
The Young Archaeologist's Field Guide	John Corcoran	Bell & Sons
The Megalithic Builders of Western Europe	Glyn Daniel	Penguin Books
Ancient Burial Mounds of England	L. V. Grinsell	Methuen
Cornish Fogous	E. V. Clarke	Methuen
Naenia Cornubiae	W. C. Borlase	
Romano-British Cornwall	Haverfield & Taylor	Victoria County History
Field Guide to Archaeology in Britain	Eric S. Wood	Collins
Christian Antiquities of Camborne	A. C. Thomas	Warne
The Saints of Cornwall	Doble ed. Attwater	Dean and Chapter Truro Cathedral
Development Survey of Cornwall		Cornwall County Council
An Introduction to the Geology of Cornwall	R. M. Barton	Bradford Barton
Cornwall's Structure and Scenery	R. M. Barton	Tor Mark Press
The Principal Antiquities of the Land's End District	A. C. Thomas & P. Pool	Cornwall Archaeological Society
The Principal Antiquities of the Newquay-Padstow District	ed. F. Nankivell	Cornwall Archaeological Society

Proceedings of the West Cornwall Field Club

Cornish Archaeology, journal of the Cornwall Archaeological Society (published annually)

The Journals of the Royal Institution of Cornwall contain valuable archaeological matter over a period of 100 years of issues.

Advent, 72
Alex Tor, 34
Amalveor, 43
Amphora, 72, 73, 93
Arrowheads, Beaker and Bronze, 21
——, Neolithic, 19
Astragalus, 76
Athelstan, 96
Avebury, 20
Axeheads, Beaker, 22
——, Flat, 37, 39
——, Neolithic, 19
——, Paleolithic, 18
——, Ritual, 37
Barrows, 30
——, Bell, 32
——, Bowl, 32
——, Building, 32
——, Cremation at, 35
——, Disc, 32
——, Excavation of, 34
——, Long, 33
——, Round, 32
——, Types, 32
Bar Lug (Lip) Pottery, 94
Baulk, 34
Bartine Castle, 67
Beaker, 22
—— Folk, 21
Bedruthan Steps, 67
Beehive Hut, 72
Beer Head, 18
Belerion, 76
Beowulf, 35
Bleu Bridge, 88
Bodmin, 68
—— Moor, 15, 44, 82
Bodrifty, 20, 45, 72, 74
Boleigh, 75
Boscastle, 95
Boscawen Un, 27
Boscregan, 36
Bosence, 88
Bosullow Trehyllys, 74
Bosvargus, 42
Brane, 26
Breage, 81, 82, 89
Brocagnus, 88, 89

Bronze, 30, 36
Bronze Age Barrows, 30
—— Barrow Building, 32
—— Barrow Cremation, 35
——, Types, 32
——, Excavation, 34
——, Domestic Sites, 44
——, Early B.A., 36
——, Late B.A., 42
——, Middle B.A., 36
Bron Gelly, 32
Brown Willy, 45
Brychan, 88
Bucket Urn, 42
Bude, 30
Budock, 81
Bulb of Percussion, 17
Burials, Primary, 34, 39
——, Secondary, 34, 39
" Bury ", 67
Cadson Bury, 67
" Car ", " Caer ", 67
Caer Bran, 68
Caerhayes, 81
Caerwynnen Quoit, 24
Callington, 21, 96
Camborne, 82
Camel, River, 68, 80, 82, 86, 88, 95, 97
Camp, 67
Cape Cornwall, 42
Capstone, 23
Carbon, 14, 32
Carloggas, 65, 72, 73, 74, 80
Carnanton, 80
Carn Brea, 19, 68, 80
Carn Creis, 36
Carn Euny, 26, 73, 75
Carn Gloose, 42
Carn, Veryan, 90
Carnmenellis, 15
Carnsew, 88
Carvossa, 79
Castle Canyke, 68
Castle Dore, 68, 69, 73, 91
—— Stone, 91
Castle-an-Dinas, 67, 68, 79
Castle Gotha, 69

Castilly, 21
Castlewitch, 21
Chamber, Tomb, 23, 26
Chi Rho, 89
Christianity, Early, 88
Chun Castle, 24, 68
—— Quoit, 24
Chycarne, 42
Chysauster, 74
Cist, 32
Cliff Castles, 67, 69
Copper, 22, 30, 36
Conan, Bishop, 96
Courtyard Houses, 72, 73
Creed, 93
Crig-a-mennis, 38
Cromlech, 23
Crowan, 89
Cunomorus Stone, 90
Daggers, 36, 37, 38
Danes, 96
Dark Ages
——, Christianity, Early, 88
——, Church, The, 92
——, Domestic, 94
——, Irish Invasion, 86
——, Kings, Cornish, 90
——, Saxons, The, 95
——, Welsh Invasion, 86
Dawns Men, 27
" Dennis ", 67
Dennis Head, 67
Deverel-Rimbury, 42
" Din ", " Dinas ", 67
Dingerein Castle, 90
Diodorus, 75
Dozmary Pool, 18, 32, 92
Dumnonii, 75, 78, 79, 83, 95
" Dynas ", 67
Egloshayle, 68
Entrance Graves, 23, 25
——, Brane, 26
——, Pennance, 26
——, Treen, 26
Ethelred II, 94
Excalibur, 92
Exeter, 78, 82, 95
Fernacre, 27

Flint Working, 17
Fogou, 72, 74
Fowey, 68, 69
Gare, 81
Garrow Tor, 45
" Gear ", 67
Gear Sands, 92
Gereint, 90
Gerrans, 90
Gillan, 42
Glastonbury, Ware, 20, 65, 69, 72, 73
Golden, 79
Gold Herring, 73
Goonzion Downs, 34
Grampound, 79
Grass-marked Pottery, 90
Gugh (I.O.S.), 26
Gulval, 28, 88
Gunwalloe, 42
Gurnard's Head, 26, 70, 71, 72
Gwennap, 81
Gwinear, 42, 89
Gwithian, 37, 44, 45, 83, 89, 93, 94
Hartland Point, 95
Harlyn Bay, 37, 38, 66, 76
Hawk's Tor, 21
Hayle, 82, 86, 88, 89
Henge Monuments, 21
Hennet, 37
Hensbarrow Downs, 15
Helford River, 67, 79
Helsbury, 38, 43
Helston, 93
Hill Forts, 67
Hingston Downs, 96
Holsworthy, 95
Hundreds, 96
Hurlers, The, 27, 36
Hurling, 28
Hut Circles, 71
Ictis, 76
Illogan, 42
Inscribed Stones
——, Bleu Bridge, 88
——, Carnsew, 88
——, Castle Dore, 91
——, St. Clement, 87
——, Doniert, 91

——, St. Endellion, 87
——, St. Kew, 87
——, Lancarffe, 88
——, Lanteglos, 95
——, Lewannick, 87
——, Men Scryfa, 17, 90
——, Nanscowe, 88
——, Penzance, 92
Irish Invasion, 86
Iron Age
——, Burial Sites, 66
——, Civilisation and Trade, 75
——, Cliff Castles, 69
——, Courtyard Houses, 73
——, Defensive Positions, 67
——, Domestic Sites, 71
——, Finds, 48
——, Fogous, 74
——, Hill Forts, 67
Isca Dumnoniorum, 78
Iseult, 91
Isles of Scilly, 23, 26
Kenidjack Castle, 42
' Ker ', 67
Kerrowe, 28
Killibury Castle, 68
Kings, 90
——, Arthur 92
——, Doniert 91
——, Gereint 90
——, Mark, 91
——, Ricatus, 92
Knackyboy Carn, 26
Kynance Gate, 45
" Lan ", 93
Lancarffe, 88
Laneast, 93
Lanivet, 93
—— Quoit, 24
Land's End, 70, 76
Lanhydrock, 93
Lanyon Quoit, 24
Lanteglos-by-Camelford, 95
Lelant, 65, 68, 89, 92
Linkinhorne, 69
Liskey, 38
" Lithos ", 17
Lizard, The, 18, 30, 43

Loe Pool, 82
Longstones, 28
Lost Church, The, 92
Lostwithiel, 93
Ludgvan, 81
Lunettes, 37
Lunulae, 37
Lydford, 94
Lynchets, 44
Mace Head, 19
Madron, 72, 74
Maen Castle, 70
Magor, 82, 83
Maiden Castle, 78
Mawgan Porth, 94
Megalithic 23
—— Chamber Tombs, 23
—— Entrance Graves, 25
—— Standing Stones, 28
—— Stone Circles, 27
" Men ", 17
Menhirs, 28
Men-an-Tol, 17, 25, 90
Men Scryfa, 17, 90
Menheer Farm, 81, 82
Merry Maidens, 27
Merthen, 79
" Mesos ", 17
Mesolithic, 17
Microliths, 18
Minions, 27
Ministry of Public Building and
    Works, 14, 18
Monoliths, 28
Morvah, 43, 68, 24
Mount's Bay, 18
Morwenstow, 95
Mulfra Hill, 72
—— Quoit, 24, 72
Muller, 66
Mylor, 93
Nanscowe, 88
Nanstallon, 79
Neolithic, 17, 19
" Neos ", 17
Newquay, 32, 37, 70, 71
Obadiah's Barrow, 26
Ogham Script, 87

Ottery, River, 95
Padstow, 69
" Palaios ", 17
Paleolithic, 17, 18
Palstave, 39, 42
Paul, 28
Pawton Quoit, 24
Pedngwinnion Point, 42
Pelynt, 36
Penhale Sands, 92
Pennance Entrance Grave, 26
Pentewan, 65
Peristalith, 33
Petrology, 19
Phillack, 89, 93
Pipers, The, 27
Plain Street, 82
Pollen Analysis, 32
Pottery, 20
——, Bar Lug (Lip), 94
——, Bronze Age, 38
——, Dark Ages, 90, 94
——, Grass Marked, 90
——, Iron Age, 65
——, Mesolithic, 19
——, Neolithic, 19, 20
——, Roman, 79, 83
Porthmeor, 74
Porthleven, 82
Poundstock, 95
Primary Burial, 34, 39
Probus, 79, 81
Pygmies, 18
Pytheas, 75
Querns, 66
Quoits, 23
——, Caerwynnen, 24
——, Chun, 24
——, Lanyon, 24
——, Lanyon, West, 24
——, Lanivet, 24
——, Mulfra, 24
——, Pawton, 24
——, Trethevy, 23, 25
——, Zennor, 24, 25
Rapiers, 39
Redcliff Castle, 67
Redruth, 19, 68, 82, 89

Resugga Castle, 68
Ribbon Handled Urns, 38
Rillaton Barrow, 36
—— Gold Cup, 36
Roman
—— Camps, 79
—— Finds, 80
—— Living Sites, 82
—— Milestones and Roads, 81, 82
Rosecliston, 37
Rosemodress, 27
Roscarrock, 88
Rough Tor, 84
Ruan Lanihorne, 93
Rumps Point, 70, 82
Saints, 86
St. Austell, 65, 94
—— Buryan, 26, 27, 75
—— Cleer, 91
—— Clement, 87
—— Columb, 67, 68, 69
—— Dennis, 69
—— Endellion, 87, 88, 89
—— Enodoc, 80, 93
—— Erth, 80, 89, 93
—— Germans, 96
—— Gothian's Chapel, 93
—— Helen's Chapel, 89
—— Hilary, 42, 81, 82
—— Issey, 88
—— Ive, 88
—— Ives, 89
—— Just-in-Penwith, 42, 81, 82
—— Just-in-Roseland, 93
—— Keverne, 43, 66, 76
—— Kew, 67, 68, 88
—— Levan, 18
—— Mabyn, 88
—— Martin's, 26
—— Mawes, 76
—— Mawgan-in-Pydar, 65, 72, 80
—— Michael's Mount, 76, 88
—— Minver, 70
—— Neot, 32, 88
—— Pirran's Oratory, 92
—— Stephen-in-Brannel, 68
—— Teath, 88
—— Winnow, 93

Samian Pottery, 79, 83
Sancreed, 68, 73, 75
Saxons, The, 95
Secondary Burials, 34, 39
Sennen, 18
Sithney, 89
Socketed Celts, 42
Spearhead, 39
Spindle Whorls, 37, 65
Standing Stones, 28
——, Kerrowe, 28
——, Pipers, The, 27
——, Tresvennack, 28
——, Try, 28
Stannon, 27
" Stock ", 95
Stone Age
——, Axes, 19
——, Beaker Folk, 21
——, Flint Working, 17
——, Mesolithic, 18
—— Monuments, 20
——, Neolithic, 19
—— Pottery, 20
—— Sites, 19
Stone Circles, 27
——, Boscawen Un, 27
——, Fernacre, 27
——, Hurlers, The, 27
——, Merry Maidens, The, 27
——, Rosemodress, 27
——, Stannon, 27
——, Stripple Stones, 27
Stonehenge, 20, 21
" Stow ", 95
Stowe's Hill, 69
Stratton, 95
Swords, 43
Tamar, River, 95, 96
Taunton, 95
Time Scale, 16
Tin, 30, 36
—— Ingot, 76, 80
Tintagel, 81, 82, 92, 93

Tolvan Stone, 25
" Ton ", 95
Towednack, 43
Treen, 26
Tregiffian, 26
Tregear, 67, 68, 79
Trelan Bahow, 66
Trencrom, 68
Trendrine, 34
Tresvennack, 28
Trevethy, 81, 82
—— Quoit, 23, 25
Trevelgue, 32, 37
—— Head, 70, 71, 80
Trevisker, 38, 45
Trevone, 66
Trevose Head, 18
Trewey-Foage, 20, 45
Trewhiddle, 94
Treyarnon Bay, 70
Tripod Dolmen, 24
Tristran, 91
Try, 28
Tumuli, 30
Urns, 38
——, Bucket, 42
——, Deverel-Rimbury, 42
——, Ribbon Handled, 38
Ventonvedna, 38
Warbstow Bury, 67, 68
Warren Cove, 70
Watergate, 72
Welsh Invasion, 86
Wessex, 86
West Lanyon Quoit, 24
West Penwith, 14, 15, 23, 26, 44, 72, 73
West Welsh, 95, 96
Windmill Hill, 19
Woolley Barrow, 32
" Worthy ", 95
Zennor, 28, 74
—— Quoit, 24, 25

BYGONE CORNWALL: A PICTORIAL HISTORY
Edited by JOHN ROSEWARNE

Cornwall has changed greatly in the past half century or so, as is self-evident in these historic photographs of the county in another day and age. This is the first of what it is hoped will be a series of illustrated books based upon the photographic collections of the Royal Institution of Cornwall at the County Museum, Truro

Small crown quarto . *72 pages* . *75 plates* . *paperback*

THE CORNISHMAN'S HOUSE
V. M. AND F. J. CHESHER

This introduction to traditional domestic architecture in Cornwall outlines the development of Cornish homes from the earliest times to the later eighteenth century. It shows the ways in which a regional and 'vernacular' style of building evolved—a book that will appeal to all who are interested in Cornish homes of former days.

Demy octavo . *142 pages* . *45 plates and other illustrations*

AN INTRODUCTION TO THE GEOLOGY OF CORNWALL
R. M. BARTON

This book is the first detailed and balanced account of the geology of the county in a single volume. Whilst appealing primarily to students, it will prove of interest also to those who would know more of a subject that is the key to much of Cornwall's scenery and character. [Second edition].

Demy octavo . *168 pages* . *20 plates* . *4 maps*

A HISTORY OF CORNISH METHODISM
THOMAS SHAW

Methodism in Cornwall has always had a distinctive ethos, not only in the old mining areas where its chief strength lay, but also in the wide agricultural areas and in the fishing coves of its rock-bound coast. Its story, unfolded here for the first time, is a fascinating one which is of more than ordinary interest.

Demy octavo . *145 pages* . *29 plates etc.*

A HISTORY OF COPPER MINING IN CORNWALL AND DEVON
D. B. BARTON

An account of the rise and fall of copper mining in the West of England, from the pioneer days of the sixteenth century to the final decline in the closing years of the last century. [Second edition].

Demy octavo . *102 pages* . *4 plates* . *map*

D. BRADFORD   BARTON LTD.
TRURO   CORNWALL